CARMEL

BY-THE-SEA

FROM ABORIGINES TO COASTAL COMMISSION

by

Sydney Temple

with

Marguerite M. Temple
as Editorial Assistant

Sydney Temple

1st Printing March 1987
ISBN: 0-912216-32-8

Published by:

Dedicated to all those
artists and writers, citizens and city leaders
who have worked together through the years
to protect the unique heritage
of Carmel-by-the-Sea

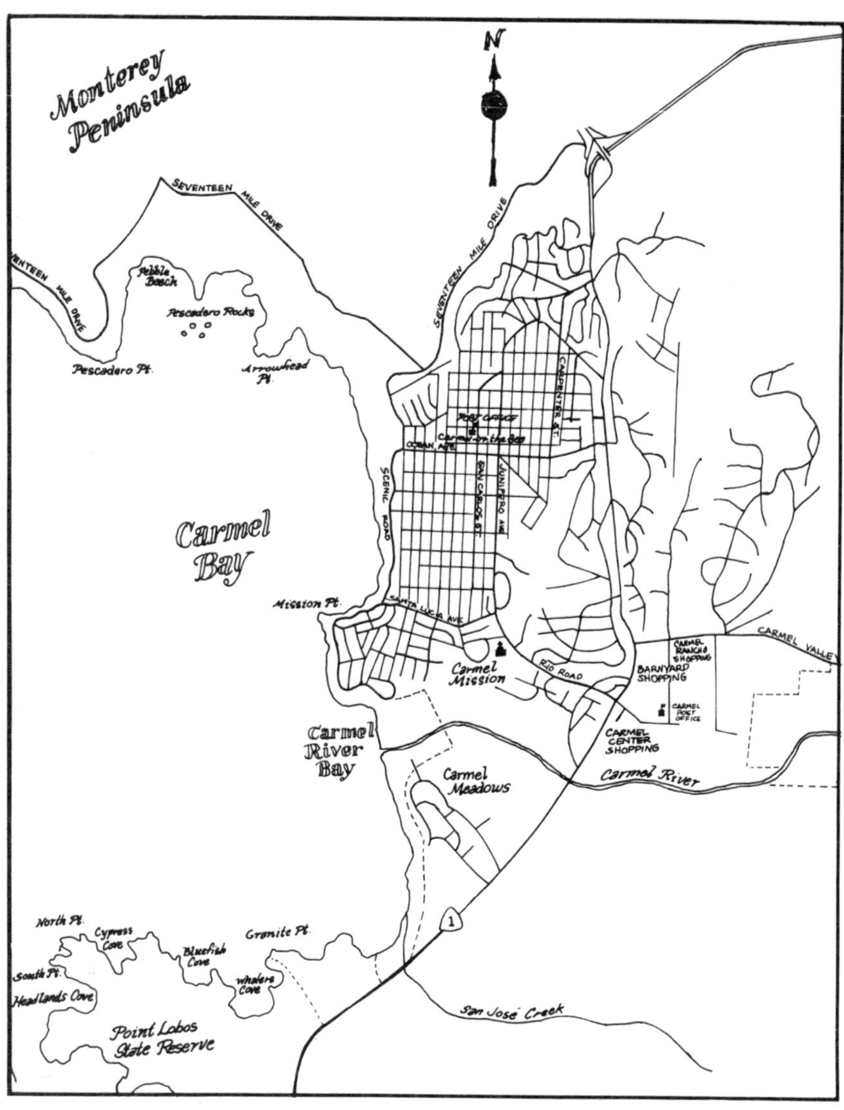

Monterey Peninsula
N
SEVENTEEN MILE DRIVE
SEVENTEEN MILE DRIVE
SEVENTEEN MILE DRIVE
Pebble Beach
Pescadero Rocks
Pescadero Pt.
Arrowhead Pt.
Carmel Bay
CARPENTER ST.
POST OFFICE
Carmel-by-the-Sea
OCEAN AVE.
SCENIC ROAD
SAN CARLOS ST.
JUNIPERO AVE
Mission Pt.
SANTA LUCIA AVE
Carmel Mission
RIO ROAD
CARMEL VALLEY
CARMEL RANCHO SHOPPING
BARNYARD SHOPPING
CARMEL POST OFFICE
CARMEL CENTER SHOPPING
Carmel River Bay
Carmel Meadows
Carmel River
1
North Pt.
Cypress Cove
Bluefish Cove
Granite Pt.
Whalers Cove
South Pt.
Headlands Cove
Point Lobos State Reserve
San José Creek

Preface

Soon after we moved to Carmel we found signs that we were living on a site formerly occupied by the area's first inhabitants. On a shelf of one of our brick walls I found a stone martar about five by three inches with a round stone resting in the cavity thereof, which may have been used as the pestle for the grinding of seeds. These items had evidently been found in the ground by a former occupant of the house and set there on the wall near the place where they were found. This was not a surprising find in this location, as I discovered, for one cannot scratch up the sand in the area of our beach frontage, between the house and the road, without coming upon broken parts of abalone shells left there by those who were preparing their meals from the molluscs that had been taken from the rocks below. The stone mortar and pestle along with the many broken abalone shells showed that our home was built upon the place once occupied by a campsite of the original inhabitants. My interest was aroused in those who had left this evidence; I wanted to know more about those who had first inhabited the place where we now lived. Since marriage my wife and I, both born in Southeren California, had lived in Illinois, Nevada, Maryland, New York, Connecticut, Massachusetts, Ontario and Hawaii, as well as for shorter times in Oxford, London and Jerusalem. Of all these places we now found that none could compare with Carmel as a place of permanent residence and I was anxious to learn how it got this way and what had been done to keep it this way. I therefore decided to discover all that I could of the history of the village from the time that the aborigines camped here to the present day.

In writing this story of Carmel, as well as the previously published history of the Carmel Mission, I have had the valuable assistance of my wife, Marguerite, as an untiring reader of the many versions through which each chapter has passed, an honest critic of what she has read and most helpful consultant on the revisions which we have made together. This Carmel story would never have been presented in its present form without the many contributions made to it by my wife and Editorial Assistant, Marguerite.

Sydney Temple
Carmel, California
1987

---

*Excavations for a house in Pebble Beach have recently unearthed the remains of an old camp of the first inhabitants of this area which, be Carbon 14 count on an abalone shell found in the midden, showed it to have been occupied more than 4,000 years agao..

CONTENTS

LIST OF ILLUSTRATIONS

Chapter VI - A Bohemia-by-the-Sea

Chapter VII - Incorporation

Chapter VIII -The Towering Poet

Chapter XII - A Heritage Town

Photographs used as designated by
Marguerite M. Temple
Other illustrations by permission of
Roger Fremier
John Livingstone
Alan McEwen
Authur McEwen
Robert W. Reese
A. A. Gray
Franklin Walker
Waldo Hicks
Steve Crouch
Gregg Wutke
Pat Hathaway Collection
Harry Downie Collection
Hank Ketcham
Joe Pierre
Lacy Williams Faia
Mrs. Wm. E. Fassett
Donnan and Garth Jeffers Collection
Judith Anderson Collection
Mrs. Marcia Kuster Rider
Mrs. Lucille Kiester
Mrs. Nadwiga Noskowisk Babcock
Bill Bates
The Carmel Pine Cone
The Monterey Herald
The Mary Austin Autobiography
The Harrison memorial Library of Carmel
The Monterey Public Library
The Monterey County Library
The Mayo Hayes O'Donnel Library
The California State Library
The Bancroft Library of the University of Calif., Berkley
The Pacific Grove Museum
The California Dept. of Parks and Recreation
The Point Lobos State Preserve
Museo Naval, Madrid

I. Aborigines along the Carmel River

The aborigines of the Carmel River Valley met a European for the first time when Sebastian Vizcaino landed on the Monterey Peninsula in 1602. He had sailed from Acapulco in Baja California on May 5 of that year with two small ships and a launch to find a good harbor for the galleons crossing the Pacific from Manilla in the Spanish Phillipines and to claim the land for the Spanish King. His ships passed the rugged mountain range which he named for Santa Lucia on December 15, Santa Lucia Day.

The river beyond the mountains he named Rio Carmelo out of respect for the three Carmelite monks who were serving as the chaplains for the expedition. It may be that the hill rising above the river reminded them of Mount Carmel in Palestine where the Carmelite Order had been founded in the 13th century. It was on Mount Carmel that Elijah defeated the prophets of Baal according to the biblical account (I Kings 18:19).

The natives that Vizcaino found to be living along the river were known as *Rumsen* called after the name of one of their settlements on the river. These were described as being rather short in stature with thick necks and round heads. It was reported that some of the men had sparse hair on the face and body while others retained full beard and facial hair. In the drawings made by early witnesses the men were pictured as being hairless because the lack of hair on face or body was considered to be ideal. The hair was removed by the use of sharp shells.

Though there was no pottery making among these people before the missionaries came, their basketry was so tightly woven that water was carried in the baskets. Bark containers were used to roast the pine nuts and grass seed which were then ground into a rough flour in stone mortars. This was moistened and rolled into balls or combined with more water to make a thick mush. Vizcaino and his men were offered such balls and mush by those they met.

The food of the natives included shellfish and other fish caught in the river as well as the flesh of deer, bear, elk and 'sea wolves' (our sea lions) and sea otters. Seafood was the staple of the diet in the summer when the members of the tribe moved to the shore. It was said that the sea wolves, for which Point lobos was later to be named, were so numerous on the water in Carmel River Bay that it looked as if one could walk out upon them, that the shores were black with sea otters and the rocky shores covered with abalone. In the winter the tribes moved back into the hills where the animals were hunted with bow and arrow. The bows were said to be rather weak because they were used only for hunting, not for war as in Europe.

A sketch of *Rumsen* natives giving an exhibiton with his hunting bow made from life by Jose Cardero who came to Carmel in 1791 (Courtesy Museo Naval, Madrid)

The *Rumsen* tribe shared a common language and customs with others of the Costanoan (Coastal) group of tribes which extended north from the Carmel River to beyond the San Francisco Bay where Sir Francis Drake had landed 23 years before the Vizcaino expedition. Francis Fletcher, Drake's chaplain, kept notes on the natives that they met and his *Notes* were included in a book published in England in 1599, *Indian Occidentalis.*

Fletcher described the aborigines he saw as "a people of tractable, free and loving nature, without guile or treachery," whose energy particularly impressed him. "The men are commonly so strong of body," he wrote, "that that which 2 or 3 of our men could hardly bear, one of them would take upon his back and without grudging carry it easily away, up hill and down hill an English mile together; they are also exceeding swift in running, and of long continuance; the use whereof is so familiar to them that they seldom go but for the most part run."

A sketch of the landing of Drake in California made by an English artist on the basis of Francis Fletcher's Notes. *Indian Occidentalis* (London, 1599)

The huts of the natives were described as consisting of a semi-circle of boughs set into the ground with the branched ends gathered at the top, forming a vault about four feet high. This allowed the light and air in at the top through the branched ends, providing natural air conditioning.

According to Fletcher the quiver for arrows was made of "fawne-skin" while the skin of elk and seals were used as the capes for the women and a sort of winter jacket for the men. He also related that "the women take a kind of bullrushes and, kembling it after the manner of hemp, make themselves thereof a loose garment being knit about their hips and so affords to them a covering of that which nature

A sketch of a *Rumsen* native made by Jose' Cardero at Carmel, showing that their dress was similar to that of the natives who met Drake as described by Francis Fletcher (Courtesy Museo Naval, Madrid)

teaches should be hidden." Regardless of nature's teaching, however, the men and children were described as wearing no clothes except for the jacket of skins about the shoulders in the winter.

The *Rumsen* family dwelling, called a *ruc*, corresponds to the hut of branches described by Francis Fletcher, except that among the *Rumsens* the vaulted top of loose branches was thatched with straw in the rainy season. A bundle of reeds was kept in the hut ready for use if unseasonable rains should threaten. In the colder winter season a fire was generally lit in the middle of the *ruc* with the smoke escaping through the loose branches above. The family would sleep on rushes and skins inside but all the grinding, food preparation, cooking and eating took place in front of the *ruc*.

Waste was simply thrown outside. When the collection of refuse became too great or the fleas became unbearable there was a form of relief which might be called "pyrocleansing." The family simply burned down the *ruc* and moved away to build a new hut of branches. When the group moved on the whole settlement was set afire and a new settlement was built on the new site. It is said that a *ruc* could be erected in about two hours.

Behind the *ruc* there was generally to be found a *temescal*, a sort of aboriginal sauna. For this a pit was dug in the ground and the *ruc* above it was made solid with thatching and covered with earth. When the *temescal* was to be used the men sat around the fire and scraped the skin with a shell or bone knife as the sweating began.

Only men entered the *temescal* and it was reported that the women and children had skin afflictions from which the men did not suffer. There was some provision for the sweat bath treatment for women but this was only practiced by the women after childbirth. At that time the new mother would dig a hole within her household *ruc* and build a ire in the depression, over whch she would place several flat stones. When the stones were hot she would cover them with green reeds and on these she would lie with the infant in her arms. When she felt the stones to be cooling she would run outside to have cold water splashed on herself and the babe. Certainly this would prepare the infant for the rough life that lay ahead.

A similar sort of "sweat box" was used for healing by both men and women. In this case a trench was dug on the beach or by the bank of the river around which fires were built. When the fire had died down the embers were raked away and the sand or soil stirred about. The person who was ill would then stretch out in trench to be covered by the heated sand. Staying there until the sweating began to cease, he or she would come out to receive the cold water treatment.

One writer has stated regarding the natives that "their body odor was said not to be offensive to whites." Certainly the use of the *temescal* with the skin scraping assured this. When the natives, unencumbered by sweat-holding clothes and recently come from a cleansing sweat-bath, met the Spanish campaigner who had marched or sailed in the same clothes for weeks without a bath or change of small clothes, the question that should be asked is whether the body odor of the Europeans was offensive to the aborigines.

A sketch of a Spanish soldier with *Rumsen* natives before a *ruc*. (Courtesy of Museo Naval, Madrid)

The dances of the men and the songs sung by the assembled natives, as reported by Fletcher, were known among the *Rumsens* for they were continued after the natives came to be connected with the missions which were to come.

The missionaries reported that the measure of their songs and dances was kept by the beat of a split stick, while a flute and pipe accompanied the songs. Bird bone whistles of the sort heard by the padres have been found in burials uncovered at settlement sites in the area.

Games played by the aborigines on the beach were also known in mission days. In the game of *takersia* a small ring of straw was tossed into the air and the competitor would hurl a rod of about five feet in length in an attempt to send it through the ring of straw. One point was scored if the straw circle was hit, two points if the rod pierced the circle. There was also a game like children's "button, button, who's got the button" In this, called *toussi*, a small stick, stone or shell was held by the member of one two-man team while the hands were hidden under a mat or skin. Then when the hands were brought out a member of the opposing team would guess the hand in which the object was held.

Vizcaino reported that though no natives were to be found living along the shore in the winter season, a great many of the aborigines did make friendly visits to the Spanish camp on the river and the country appeared to be rather thickly populated up the valley. He wrote in his report that the soil was fertile and that large pines covered the headlands while white and black poplars grew thick along the river together with many willow trees. He found the climate to be like that of Castile and the flora and fauna of the district much like that which he had known in Spain.

Because he arrived in the winter when the little river was in its flood stage he received a false impression of its importance. And when his report was taken back to New Spain (Mexico) there were those there who feared lest the French should find their way up to the headwaters of this river from their forts on the Mississippi and come down the river to make claim to the area.

Yet it was to be 167 years before a Spanish land expedition was sent to claim the land for Spain. In 1769 Charles II, fearing that the Russians would move south from their base in the Aleutian Islands or that England might still send settlers to establish the claim for the land that Drake had made in the 16th century, ordered that there be exploration north from Baja California.

Gaspar de Portola, Governor of Baja California, was appointed to lead the expedition north and Fr. Junipero Serra to accompany him to set up Franciscan missions for the purpose of "civilizing the natives." After leaving La Paz, the capital of Baja California on May 16, 1769, Portola arrived at the bay named for San Diego by Vizcaino. There he set up a military Presidio with a squad of soldiers on guard and Serra established the first Mission in Nueva California.

Because Serra's foot had become inflamed from an old wound he remained at the San Diego mission, sending his colleague Fr. Juan Crespi to accompany the Portola party as it continued north toward the great Monterey Bay which had been so flowingly described by Vizcaino. It was there at the "natural harbor" of the former explorer's description that the capital of Nueva California was to be established.

By summer the party had passed around the Santa Lucia Mountains but Portola failed to recognize the Monterey Bay which had no natural harbor. However when he moved south from the bay he found an ensenada (little bay) with an arroya (small stream) that entered the estuary through a lagoon. This same river, which Vizcaino had described as "copius river" when he had seen it in the winter flood stage, was only a small stream when it was found by Portola. This was the Carmel River which then, as now, has so small a flow

The view that Portola had when he came upon the Carmel River. (Courtesy of the Hathaway Collection)

of water in the summer that it was not recognizable as the river described by Vizcaino.

After continuing north as far as what we now know as San Francisco Bay, but which they did not consider to be of any importance, they returned to the great bay which they had not recognized before. Finding the stream south of the bay now to be a "small but copious river" they realized that they had found the place for which they were searching. Fr. Crespi celebrated mass by the river on December 3 at the site of the future Carmel Mission and village of Carmel-by-the-Sea.

On that same day they experienced the winter weather which every year drove the natives back into the valley and the hills. A heavy rain preceded the violent storm which came sweeping in from the ocean. While they waited the supplies began to run low because the small supply ships had been unable to make the voyage by the mountain range in the face of these of these storms. The members of the expedition existed for a time on pelicans and seagulls that they were able to kill, together with seeds and *pinolas* that were brought to them by the natives from upriver.

When they could wait no longer for the ships they began the return south on December 10. Portola had two large crosses erected as signals to the ships should they arrive later. One was set on the hill rising above the river and the other on Monterey Bay near the place the ships might anchor. In 1944 similar crosses were erected at these two sites by Hary Downie to mark the 175th anniversary of the raising of the Portola crosses. The one erected by Downie on the sand dune on Monterey Bay still stands but the cross above the Carmel River was blown down in the great storm of 1983. It has now been replaced by interested Carmelites, strengthened by a large angle iron set in a concrete base.

On the trip south the members of Portola's party lived on the flesh of their pack mules and the gifts of food provided by natives in the country through which they passed. Reaching San Diego in January the Governor found that food was dangerously low because no other supply ships had arrived from San Blas in his absence. By March he had decided to close the San Diego Presidio and Mission as he prepared the whole expedition for the return overland to San Blas. At the urging of Serra and Crespi he held out for a while longer and the ships did arrive from the south to save the California exploration.

By April of 1770 preparations were completed for another foray to Monterey Bay and the Carmel River. The condition of his foot and leg forced Serra to board the packetboat *San Antonio* for the voyage while Crespi again went with Governor Portola on the 460 mile march north. The land party arrived back at the bay and Carmel River ahead of the ship which was fighting headwinds along the rocky shore. There Crespi found that the cross erected previously on the rise above the river was surrounded by feather-tipped arrows struck in the ground and heavy stakes, on one of which a string of not-so-fresh sardines and pieces of flesh were hung. Scattered around were heaps of clams.

The arrows and the food at the foot of the cross suggested that the natives had left them as a sign of veneration for the religious symbol, so might be taken as a good omen for the future success of the missionaries. This

Portola's Cross as it appeared to the Natives. (Photograph by Marguerite Temple, prepared by Filmcraft, Carmel, California)

was to be borne out by later witness given to Crespi by the natives. He was to write in the diary that he kept, "when the neophytes (converted natives) spoke Spanish well enough to be understood they on various occasions explained that the first time they saw our men they noticed that everyone wore on his breast a small glittering cross; that when the Spaniards had gone away and left this large cross on the shore they dreaded to approach the sacred sign because at night they would see it surrounded by brilliant rays which would dispel the darkness; that the cross appeared to grow larger so as to reach to the skies; that in the daytime, when it stood in its natural size without the rays, they would approach it and offer meat, fish and mussels in order to enlist its favor, lest it should harm them, and that, when to their amazement they saw that it did not consume those things, they would offer their plumes and arrows in token of their desire to be at peace with the people who planted it there."

Upon their return to their former camp site on the river the members of the expeditionary force were greeted by some 40 or 50 natives bearing feather-tiped rods and baskets of *pinolas* as gifts. Soon thereafter the chief arrived to welcome the returning forces of Spaniards, his face and body painted a shining black. Crespi was to report in his diary that this was the color of welcome among the *Rumsen* people. There was no longer any doubt about the welcome that the aborigines of the Carmel Valley extended to the new arrivals.

With the lightening of the winds the packetboat *San Antonio* was able to make its way north, bringing supplies and the other members of the expedition. When the ships were sighted fires were lit on the dunes of Monterey Bay as signals and Portola came from the Carmel River to greet the new arrivals. He led Fr. Serra and others of the ship's party back to the camp on the river where they were greeted by a large group of natives, now settled in a summer settlement nearby.

The arrivals were welcomed with the gift of three deer and many baskets of *pinolas.* That hospitality at the riverside by the aborigines was to be repeated in future years as many visitors were welcomed at the Carmel Mission and the village of Carmel-by-the-Sea.

Though the place on the Carmel River was found by Portola, and by many people since that day, to be the most attractive area for settling, the ships were much better off in the shallower water beyond the point of the Monterey Peninsula. Off the Monterey and Carmel shores is one of the world's deepest ocean valleys, reaching a depth of over a mile. Sand from the Salinas River flow has shallowed much of Monterey Bay so that anchoring in the bay is possible. The little Carmel River Bay, on the other hand, has a depth of 600 feet close to land and has been found to descend to a depth of 3,000 to 4,000 feet opposite the mouth of this river, making anchoring difficult.

The land at the mouth of the Carmel River is much more welcoming than the sea which retains a very low temperature close to the beach due to the movement of the cold water from the great depths close to the shore. Moreoever the steep drop just beyond the water line makes swimming especially dangerous in the Carmel River Bay. Just in the years between 1971 and 1980 there were 27 swimming-related deaths between Carmel Point and Whaler's Cove in Point Lobos. Though the Carmel-by-the-Sea beach north of Carmel Point is safer for swimming, great care must be taken by all who swim in the frigid waters off these shores. This was the reason why the *Rumsen* natives, while being expert hunters in the wooded mountains, were not great swimmers or boatmen, doing their fishing and mollusc gathering from the safety of the shore.

Bibliographical Notes

Records of Vizcaino and Crespi are to be found in English translation in *Spanish Exploration of the Southwest, 1542-1706* by Professor Herbert E. Bolton (University Press, Berkeley, Calif., 1959). Extracts from the "*Notes*" of Francis Fletcher published in *The World Encompassed by Sir Francis Drake* are to be found conveniently collected in *Elizabethan California* by Professor Robert F. Heizer, Appendix II (Ballena, Romona, Calif., 1974). See also *The Costanoan Indians* by the same author (De Anza College, 1974). The journeys of Portola in 1969 were reported in his Journal which is to be found in English translation in the *Publications of the Academy of Pacific Coast History* for the years 1910 and 1911.

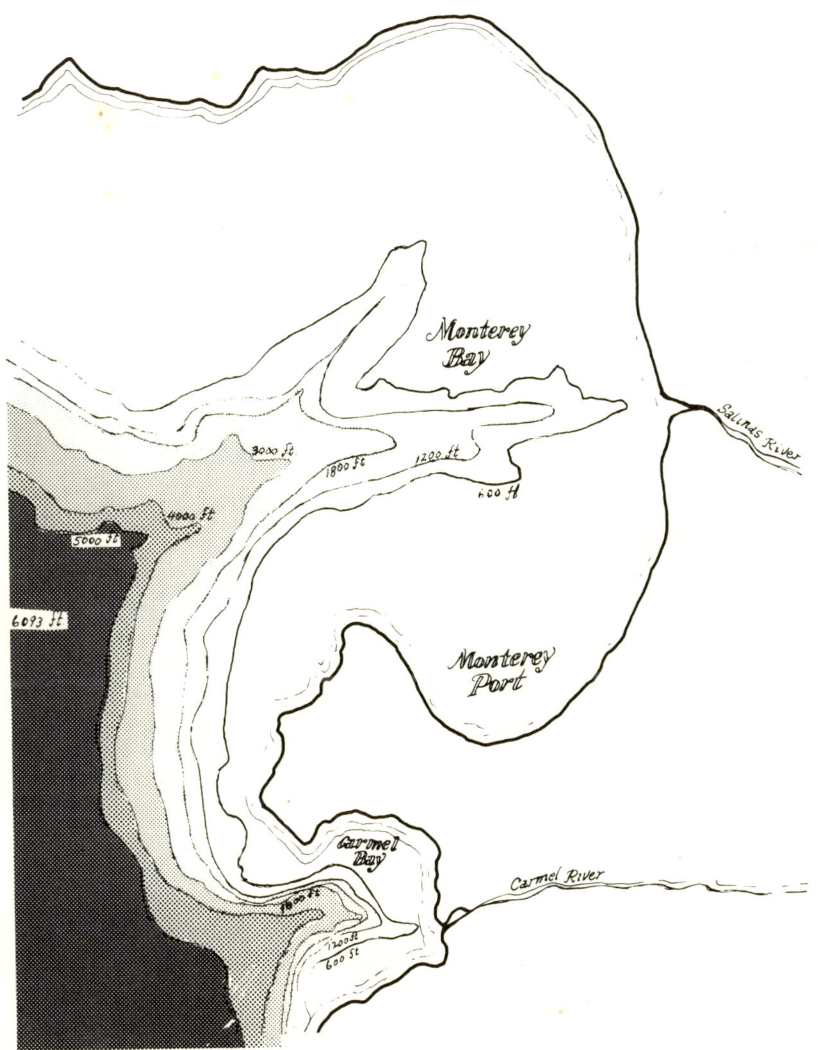

A map of the water depths in Monterey Bay and Carmel Bay, based on the model in the Pacific Grove Museum. (Map by Joe Pierre)

II. San Carlos Mission Rises by the River.

Father Junipero Serra, the Padre-Presidente of the Franciscan Missions in all of California, landed from the packetboat *San Antonio* on the shore of Monterey Bay on May 31, 1770. The land party under Governor Portola, which had arrived a week earlier, had set up camp by the Carmel River for the officers and left a squad of soldiers on the shore of the bay to keep small open fires burning as signals to the expected ship. When the ship was sighted word was sent to the river camp and Portola with his officers came over the hill to welcome the new arrivals. As soon as he came ashore Fr. Serra celebrated mass for the assembled exploration parties.

Miguel Jose Serra, who was born at Petra on the Spanish island of Mallorca on November 12, 1713, had taken on the religious name Junipero in the Franciscan Order after Brother Junipero, a close friend and faithful follower of St. Francis, founder of the Order. At the age of twenty-three Father Serra had occupied the Chair of Philosophy at Lullian University at Palma on Mallorca.

He had come to New Spain in1749 with a group of Franciscan missionaries that included two of his pupils from the Lullian University, Fr. Juan Crespi and Fr. Francisco Palou, both of whom were to be associated with him at the Carmel Mission until his death. It was after twenty years of service in missionary activity on the mainland of New Spain that Junipero Serra, at the age of fifty-six, began the greatest task of his life, the bringing of Christianity and with it civilization to California from the center on the Carmel River.

Because the settlement on the Monterey Bay was to be the new capital of California, Serra first established the Mission there in connection with the military Presidio. The Mission was named for San Carlos Borromeo, the patron saint of King Charles III, the Mission church serving as the Presidio chapel. The church which was to be built on the site was designated a 'royal chapel' and today serves as the Cathedral for the Diocese of Monterey.

Serra soon realized that the location of the Mission adjacent to the Presidio on Monterey Bay was not ideal and applied to the authorities in Mexico City for permission to move it to the Carmel River location, six miles to the south. The proposed move was desirable for two reasons: to have neophytes, as converted natives were known, farther away from the bad influence of the soldiers of the Presidio, and to locate the Mission in a place suited to the agriculture which must be developed to support the expected number of neophytes and to provide for the needs of the Presidio. And perhaps there was a third reason for the move to the Carmel Valley; a biographer of Serra wrote, "the Padre-Presidente was sensitive to the beauty of nature and there is hardly a more beautiful spot to be found on earth than the green vale of the Carmelo."

When the permission was received for the transfer of the Mission from the location on Monterey Bay to the Carmel River site the Padre-Presidente moved from the Presidio to a brush hut near a native settlement on a small hill overlooking the river. He began to build the Carmel Mission with his own hands in the summer of 1771. As helpers in the building he had forty 'neophytes' who had come with them from Baja California, three soldiers from the Presidio and five sailors who had remained behind when the *San Antonio* had sailed south with Governor Portola aboard. Outside his hut Serra first erected a great cross around which daily services were held.

A sketch of the early buildings at the Carmel Mission surounded by a stockade with the *rucs* of the native *rancheria* in the background. (Courtesy of the Downie Collection)

This cross, which was still standing in the midst of the Mission compound when Vancouver visited there in 1792, was replaced in 1940 in its original form and location by Harry Downie in rebuilding the Carmel Mission. There it is to be seen today, standing within the mission patio just outside the Museum entrance.

The first buildings at *Rio Carmelo*, like those in Monterey, were built of logs stuck into the ground to form the walls with other logs laid across the top. On these horizontal logs there was a mat of sticks and a covering of turf to form the primitive, and not very waterproof, roof.

Fr. Palou, in his biography of Serra, described the first buildings as consisting of "one room for a chapel, to which was added a dwelling of four rooms and a larger room for a granary, besides a house for keeping the boys and a kitchen. All these structures were of wood and had a flat roof, and all were surrounded by a stockade. At one corner of the stockade a house was built for the guards and within sight some corrals for the mules and cattle were erected." The Mission San Carlos Borromeo in its new location was rededicated on Christmas Eve, 1771.

The livestock at the Mission consisted of a boar and a sow with four pigs that had been brought over from the Presidio in Monterey, plus nine cows with calf, two yearling heifers and six heifer calves driven up from San Diego as the normal allowance for a new Mission. To these were soon added a bull that was sent as a personal gift to Serra from the Padres at the San Diego Mission. It was intended that the missions would develop sufficient herds and agricultural crops to supply the adjacent Presidios. But in the early years of the Spanish extension into Nueva California this appeared to be a forlorn hope.

One year after the establishment of the Carmel Mission there arose the possibility that all the Missions of Nueva California together with the Presidios would have to be abandoned, for they were entirely dependent on ships from Baja California. And captains feared to sail up the Baja and Nueva California coasts in the winter months because of the gales encountered along the mountainous shores. Those who did attempt the passage were often driven back by the wintry winds.

Captain Fages, commander of the Monterey Presidio, in order to save the situation, took a contingent of soldiers on a hunting expedition to a valley in the south whch was famous as a haunt for bears, near the present location of San Luis Obispo. Fages was successful in the hunt and was able to send 25 loads of jerked bear meat to the Carmel Mission after keeping enough to provide for the needs of the Presidio.

The second great famine came in 1774 while Serra was away in Mexico City convincing the new Viceroy that the California mission enterprise should be continued and expanded. Fr. Palou, who was in charge of the Mission in Serra's absence, wrote of that time, "The worst kind of famine that was ever endured in the regions around Monterey visited us. For eight months milk was the manna for all from the Commandante and Fathers down to the least individual and I shared it with the rest . . . At the mission of San Carlos for thirty seven days we were without a tortilla or as much as a crumb of bread. The meals consisted of *garvanzos* (a type of local bean) ground to flour with which milk was mixed." Another reported, however, that "They did not mind the famine nearly as much as they did the absence of snuff, which seems to have run out in November '73." So problems with tobacco are not new.

A year later Don Juan Bautista de Anza arrived in the region after an overland trek from Sonora in northern New Spain with a party of 240 including 20 families of farmers as settlers. They brought with them 500 horses, 350 head of cattle and a pack train of 165 mules laden with household goods and agricultural tools. Arriving on March 10, 1776, de Anza left most of his party at the Presidio. He accepted the invitation of the Padres to stay at the Mission himself and his gift of cattle greatly increased the mission herds. This

The reenactment of the de Anza trek from Sonora to California as the party came to Carmel on March 10, 1976, (Courtesy of the Hathaway Collection)

historic journey of de Anza's was reenacted on the bicentennial anniversary of the trek from Sonora in New Mexico to California with relays of participants following the original trail. They were welcomed at the rebuilt Mission San Carlos Borromeo on March 10, 1976.

Father Pedro Font, de Anza's chaplain, left this description of the neophytes and the mission garden: "The Indios of this Mission who already number 400 Christians appeared to me to be rather tractable . . . They devote themselves to fishing, for at this place many good fish are caught. Besides the sardines, which are plentiful, there are also many good salmon which enter the river to spawn. Of this fish we ate almost every day we were here . . . I went for a walk through the garden full of cauliflower, lettuce and other vegetables and herbs. And the finest thing about that country is that without irrigation all such vegetables are raised, than which there are no better in Mexico . . . In short, although all the rest of the Missions are very good, this one seems to me to be the best of all."

By 1783 enough land had been cleared to provide vegetables for the 700 persons living at the Mission and for the village of Monterey that was growing around the Presidio. An irrigation canal had been extended from the river to a pool for the keeping of fish, conveniently located near the Mission enclosure. There were 520 head of cattle, 82 horses, 20 mules, and 25 pigs in addition to the flocks of sheep on the Mission lands.

The natives were trained as plowmen, shepherds and *vaqueros*, horseback-riding cattle herders, as well as blacksmiths and carpenters. Adobe bricks of the native clay formed into cubes and dried in the sun were made by the neophytes and used for the buildings while roof tiles were hand formed and baked pottery-hard in the Mission kilns. Workshops at the nine Missions that Serra had founded by that date provided most of what was needed for California life including rough furniture and simple agricultural tools. The Mission San Carlos Borromeo now consisted of a new adobe church, a three-room priest's residence, which Downie duplicated in the present museum complex, two barns and thirty workshops in addition to the quarters for the neophytes.

On August 28, 1784, four days before his 79th birthday,

Junipero Serra died in his cell at the Carmel Mission where a restoration of the cell stands today. Father Palou, the fellow Mallorcan who had been a companion of Serra's since the days that Serra had taught him Philosophy at the Lullian University, was at his bedside. In compliance with Serra's wishes his body was interred in the sanctuary of the adobe

The figure of Junipero Serra with a model of the Carmel mission church in his left hand which stands in Statuary Hall in the Capital building in Washington D. C.

church next to his other beloved companion, Fr. Juan Crespi who had died two years earlier. When the adobe church was replaced with a stone church in 1793, the new one was built over the same area as the former with the sanctuary so placed that the burial places of the two Franciscan Padres were within the altar rail of the new church where they are to be seen today.

As one of the giants of California history, a representation of Junipero Serra stands in the Sanctuary Hall of the nation's Capital Building as a representative of this state. The figure, standing with the cross held high in the right hand, well expresses the contribution that Serra made to California history. In the left hand is held a model of the Carmel Mision church, bringing Carmel's presence into the center of our nation.

Fr. Palou, who succeeded Serra as Padre-Presidente, soon applied for permission to retire to the Missionary College in Mexico City, there to write a history of the California Missions and a biography of Junipero Serra. When permission was granted and Palou prepared to leave California, the one selected as the next Padre-Presidente was another who had come to New Spain with Serra and Palou, Fr. Fermin de Lasuen.

Under the direction of Fr. Lasuen, the San Carlos Mission had its greatest growth and the number of missions in California doubled. It was in those years that a series of foreign visitors came to the Carmel Mission, each leaving his impression of the Mission in words and pictures, through which it is possible to follow the development of the Mission on the bank of the Carmel River.

The first of these European visitors sailed into Monterey Bay in 1786 and soon came over the hill to the Carmel Mission. Jean Francois de Galaup, Compte de la Perouse, a scientist and experienced seaman, had sailed from Brest on a world-wide voyage of exploration for the French Government. Like visitors before and after him La Perouse was impressed with the countryside. He observed that while his own native land had fertile soil, "The fertility of the Pacific Coast was something which no European farmer could imagine."

He reported that, "The deer were almost tame and even the whales gambolled and spouted in the sea with a pleasant show of familiarity and a complete absence of fear." But his greatest enthusiasm was reserved for the missionaries and the generosity of the Spanish Government in supporting their efforts half a world away, "that have no other purpose than the conversion and civilization of the Natives, and that yield no profit unless God be the paymaster."

La Perouse, for all his enthusiasm for the land and the support being given to the missionary enterprise by the Spanish Government, was not blind to the difficulties with which the missionaries in California were faced, commenting, "the enthusiasm of religion, with the reward that it promises, can alone compensate for the sacrifice, the disgust, the fatigue and the danger which the missionary life entails."

A view of the Carmel mission compound in 1786 with the natives drawn up opposite the French soldiers at the reception of La Perouse. (Courtesy of the Downie Collection)

Anxious to leave a 'small contribution' for life at the Mission, the French explorer presented the Padres with seed potatoes and fruit tree sprouts from Chili as well as many containers of vegetable seeds brought with him from France. It was also reported that a 'semi-portable' flour mill was left by the Frenchman but there is no evidence that it was ever used, the native women preferring their primitive stone mortar and pestle for the milling of their seeds. There are today two millstones in the cemetery at the side of the Mission church which show no signs of wear and it has been suggested that these unused stones may be the remains of the 'semi-portable flour mill' left by Perouse.

The next visitor to have left his impressions of the Carmel Mission was the Italian Captain Alejandro Malaspina who was on a globe circling expedition under the auspices of the Spanish Government. He arrivd at the San Carlos Mission on September 20, 1791. He reported to his Government that the arrival of the Spaniards in California had brought to the people, "without the slightest spilling of blood, the end of a thousand local wars that were destroying them" to be replaced with "social beginnings and a holy religion."

A year after the visit of Malaspina there was to arrive at the Carmel Mission the first English visitor, Captain George Vancouver. Coming to "New Albion", as he insisted on using the name given to the region by Sir Francis Drake in 1579, his ships arrived in Monterey Harbor at the end of November, 1792. With his fellow officers he came over the hill and was "handsomely entertained" at dinner in an outdoor bower set up to handle the large party. As part of the entertainment for the visitors the neophytes gave a demonstration of their hunting technique which was much admired according to the records kept by the English captain.

Vancouver reported that preparations were being made for the permanent stone church that was to be built on the site of the adobe structure which had been removed to make way for it. Manuel Estevan Ruiza, who had been brought from Mexico City to build the stone church in Monterey, had come over to build the Carmel Mission church when he had completed his work there. Having built the church at San Blas in Baja California and many other churches throughout New Spain, he designed the Monterey and Carmel churches according to the 'Spanish style' which had been established, making the plans as he went along. Some years later the stone valt of the ceiling collapsed except the portion above the sanctuary. When Downie replaced the vaulted ceiling with wood and plaster he kept the original form and painted it to preserve the 'curious effect' of the original stone construction.

A view of the completed Carmel Mission with the stone church in the center with worshops and dormitories for the single neophytes adjoining and houses for the neophyte families on the hill to the right. (Courtesy of the downie Collection)

When Fr. Lasuen died in 1803 the California economy was based on the 233,000 head of cattle that were run on the Mission lands throughout California. Hides and tallow from the cattle were traded for goods which were brought by trading ships that were beginning to come to the California ports in ever increasing numbers. The first American 'tourist' to leave an account of his trip to Carmel was John Henry Dana who arrived in 1835 as a member of the crew on a trading vessel from Boston.

In his book *Two Years Before the Mast* he described in some detail the village of Monterey, calling it "decidedly the pleasantest and most civilized place in California." But of the Carmel Mission he left only the record of a meal that he was given after a horseback ride over the hill on a Sunday. "Toward noon we procured horses," he wrote, "and rode out to the Carmel Mission which is about a league from the town, where we got something in the way of dinner -- beef, eggs, frijoles, tortillas and some middling wine -- from the major-domo who, of course, refused to make any charge as it was the Lord's gift, yet received our present, as a gratuity, with a low bow, touch of the hat, and '*Dios se lo pague*'."

Dana's simple account of a meal at Mission San Carlos Borromeo is notable because it was to prove to be the last report that we have of the Carmel Mission hospitality before secularization and sale was to leave it, along with the other California Missions, as a ruin.

It was the very success of the Missions that led to their destruction. The Padres had opened the great expanse of land on the Pacific Coast to farming and pasteurage and it was the possession of this that came to be sought by the governments first of Spain, then of Mexico.

The first threat came in 1813 in which year an act as passed in the Spanish Cortes (Legislative Assembly) that all Missions in America were to be handed over to the secular authorities. One-half of the Mission land was to be divided among the native converts and the other half sold to help to pay Spain's national debt. Fortunately for the California Missions, the bishops of New Spain did not have enough secular priests to take the place of the Padres in the Missions so the Act of Secularization was not implemented in California.

After Mexico gained its independence from Spain the threat to the valued properties and possessions of the California Missions became greater. The Missions, being responsible for the support of the government Presidios, were providing the equivalent of $16,000 worth of supplies each year. For this support the missionaries were issued promissory notes on the government which were proving to be worthless.

When the outstanding notes owed to the Missions of California amounted to more than $500,000, it became evident that only by the seizure of the Mission property and assets under the guise of secularization could the Mexican government avoid the payment of its obligations. The fate of the Missions in California was sealed.

In 1833 the Mexican Congress ordered the secularization of all California Missions and on November 3, 1834 Mexico's California Assembly authorized the confiscation of all the Mission properties. But it was not until 1844 that Governor Manuel Micheltorena, the last California

Governor to be sent from Mexico, decreed that all Mission lands should be sold and the money used for the defensive forces of Mexico. It was the looming threat of war with the United States which brought about the final act.

The dates of January 2, 3 and 4 of 1846 were set for the auctioning of the Carmel Mission and its lands. William Garner, a builder of Monterey, bought the Mission buildings to use the materials from the ruins for his projects there. Some of the old adobe houses that still stand in Monterey were constructed of timbers and roof tiles taken from the destroyed buildings of the Carmel Mission.

The roofless church of the Carmel Mission with only the stone walls and stone tower standing. (Courtesy of the Hathaway Collection)

Bibliographical Notes

Father Palou had written of the life of Fr. Serra during his last years in California under the title, "*Relacion Historica de la Vida y Apostolicas Tareas_del Venerable Padre Junipero Serra*". This was published in Mexico City in 1787. After his retirement to the Franciscan headquarters in Mexico City he wrote *Noticias de la California* based on documents and notes that he had kept from the time that the Franciscans arrived at Loreta in Baja California. This was sent to Madrid but was not published until 1857 when it was included as four volumes of *Documentos para Historia de Mexico.* both of these have appeared in English versions as translated in 1926 by Professor Herbert E. Bolton, the latter under the title, *Historical Memoirs of New California* (University Press, Berkeley, Calif.)

An English translation of Fr. Crespi's Journals was offered the next year by Professor Bolton under the title, *Crespi, Missionary-Explorer, 1769-1774.* In 1930 appeared his *Anza's California Expedition* which includes the translation of the diary of Fr. Font.

A brief bibliography which provides the basis for the further study of the missions and missionaries of California is to be found in *Mission to Paradise, The Story of Junipero Serra and the Missions of California* by Kenneth M. King, F.I.A.L. (Franciscan Herald Press, 1956/75). Other recent works include *The Life and Times of Junipero Serra* by M.J. Geiger, O.F.M. (Acad. of American Franciscan History, 1959), *Mission San Carlos Borromeo, The Father of the Missions* by Zephyrin Engelhardt, O.F.M. (Ballena Press, 1973), and *The Carmel Mission, From Founding to Rebuilding* by Sydney Temple (Valley Publishers, 1980).

III. Ranchos Fill the Mission Lands

The first division of the lands of the Carmel Mission was made early in 1794 when the California Governor, Diego de Borica, granted an 'occupancy permit' for land on the Salinas River to Joaquin Ysidro Castro and his son-in-law Jose Maria Sobranes. Castro had brought his family overland to California in 1776 with the de Anza Expedition, while his son-in-law had been one of the twenty soldiers in Portola's party in 1770 and was subsequently stationed at the Carmel Mission as one of the guards. This 'occupancy permit' was granted to these pioneers with the understanding that all the lands belonged to the natives connected with the Mission, the Franciscan Padres having no possessions in accordance with their vow of poverty. The land was to be held by Castro and Soberanes at the sufferance of the missionaries and was to be vacated if the Mission desired to have the land returned.

But when the aging Padre, Fr. Fermin Francisco de Lasuen, tested the provisions in 1802 by demanding that the land be put again under the control of the Mission, the land was granted outright to the Castros and Soberanes by the then Governor, Jose Joaquin de Arrillaga. This established the principal by which large grants of Mission lands were made to veterans and others for the establishment of ranchos on the former Mission lands.

The first rancho grant in the Carmel Valley and by far the largest was one of 26,581 acres at the headwaters of the river, some fourteen miles inland. This grant was made to Rafael Gomez who named his expanse the *Rancho los Tularcitos,* Little Tule-reeds Ranch, for the Tularcitos Creek which ran through his land.

The second grant in the Carmel region was for land about fifteen miles down the coast from the Carmel River mouth. That 8,949-acre spread, appropriately named *Rancho el Sur,* The South Ranch, was granted in the same year by Governor Jose Figuroa to Juan Bautista Alvarado. Alvarado was another of the twenty soldiers who accompanied Portola on his first trip north. Located on the hillside pastures extending back from the shore, the rancho extended from what came to be called the 'Little Sur', 'Little South' River to the 'Big Sur' River. For many years the region could only be reached by a long and hazardous horseback ride.

A year after these two grants Governor Figueros granted the 8,814 acres of the *Rancho San Francisquito* , Little St. Francis Ranch, to Esteban Munras, a prominent citizen of Monterey and former *alcalde,* mayor. Munras had come from Spain in 1812 to open a trading house in California's capital. The Munras Memorial Museum, set on the grounds of the Carmel Mission, was dedicated in 1961 by the donor, a fourth generation Munras heir, Maria Antonia Field.

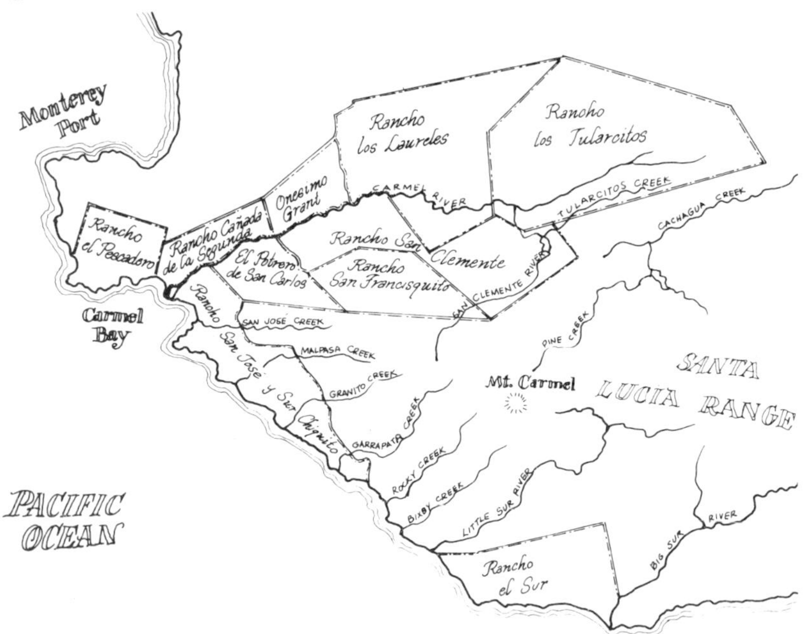

Ranchos in the Carmel Valley and to the south of the river mouth, as originally granted. (Map by Joe Pierre)

Exhibited in the small museum, set behind the Mission Church, are materials collected from the Valley Ranchos and from the Munras family since Esteban Munras came in 1812. The diary that Munras kept on his journey is to be seen along with the Spanish land grants of several of the ranchos and the patents issued by the U.S. Attorney General after California was made a part of the United States. The registration for the ear-mark and brand used on the *Rancho San Francisquito* are on display as well a the branding iron used.

There one may view an authentic recreation of the principal room of the Munras town house of that time with the original marble mantle brought around the horn from Spain in 1842. The period furnishings of the room include a cradle and child's furniture made by a carpenter at the Monterey Presidio. Clothes worn by the ladies of the Munras family in the Spanish and Mexican periods are also on display.

Though it was decreed by the Secularization Act that one half of the Mission land was to go to converted natives, only a small percentage ever came into their possession. This small portion was distributed as small farm plots given to some of the Mission neophytes. The great majority of the *Rumsens* who had been at the Mission were to serve as *vaqueros,* cattlemen, for the absentee ranch owners or as laborers and servants for the Spanish families in Monterey.

The only sizable grant made to any of the neophytes of the Carmel Mission was a tract of 4,592 acres granted to Juan Onesimo, his daughter Loretta and her husband Domingo Peralta. Juan Onesimo, who had worked on the building of the Mission Church as a boy, had grown up in the Mission. Before the place was abandoned Onesimo had served as the accompanyist for the mass on the violin which the Padres had taught him to play. He took his violin with him when the Mission buildings were sold and today it is back in a case in the rebuilt Padre's rooms at the Mission.

In 1839 the last unclaimed land in the valley, the 6,625 acre *Rancho los Laureles*, The Laurel Bush Ranch, was granted to Jose Manuel Boronda, the son of a corporal in the Mexican army. In the next year Boronda repaired an adobe building of three rooms and moved his family into the valley as the first rancho owner to live on his rancho apart from Juan Onesimo and the Peraltas. The Boronda adobe, now somewhat remodelled and completely modernized, is still used as a residence in the heart of the valley.

The Boronda Adobe, still standing in the Carmel Valley. (Courtesy of the Monterey Library)

Dona Juana Boronda proved to be a good neighbor to the Onesimo-Peralta family and continued to do all in her power to defend them from the schemes of Antonio Romero, the civil administrator, who was determined to take the Onesimo grant for his own. Those native land owners were able for a time, with the help of the Borondas, to hold their land, enjoying the great rounds of cheese sent over to them from time to time by Dona Joana.

Things took a turn for the worse, however, in 1841 when Domingo Peralta's dead body was discovered in a ravine in the hills. It looked for a time that Loretta Peralta, with her small children, would not be able to keep the rancho and, after losing it, would have to become a house servant in Monterey like so many of the other *Rumsen* natives.

A British seaman, James Meadows, who had jumped ship at Monterey, was to prove to be the savior of the Peralta family and the Peralta lands. Domingo and Loretta Peralta had hidden Meadows on their rancho in the valley far from the search crew. After helping for a time on the Onesimo grant the seaman had acted as a *vaquero* for the absentee owner of the *Rancho el Sur.*

When Meadows heard of Loretta's troubles he went to her aid and was successful in holding off Antonio Morena and in keeping the rancho in her hands. Within a year he had married Loretta and when California became a part of the United States he was able to get the patent on the land which then came to be known as the "Meadows Tract". James Meadows became a leader of those who were beginning to move into the valley and was instrumental in getting a school established there. He gave the land for the school, helped to build the schoolhouse and made the furniture to go into it. Among the pupils at this first Carmel school were the children of Loretta -- Isabella and her four brothers.

Isabella Meadows, born on July 7, 1846, the day

that Commander Sloat accepted the surrender of Monterey, was to be the instrument for the preservation of the record of the *Rumsen* natives of the Carmel area. Fascinated by the stories told by her mother and father, she learned the *Rumsen* language and sought out knowledge of the people who still worked their small holdings in the river valley. In 1925, at the age of eighty-nine, she was brought to the Smithsonian Institute in Washington, D.C., in order that her knowledge might be preserved for the future. She made records which are now available for any who want knowledge about the *Costanoan* natives and the sub-tribe *Rumsen*.

Carmel's first school, the Carmel School on the Meadow's Tract with the teacher and her first class. (Courtesy of the Mayo Hayes O'Donnel Library)

Rumors of gold in the mountains, based on native legends that had circulated around the Carmel Mission for most of its existence, were revived after the '49 gold strike to the north. A report in the

Monterey newspaper in 1869 that $100,000 in gold had been taken from the Los Burros region in the Santa Lucia Mountains brought many gold seekers to that area between Cape San Martin and the town of Jolon high in the mountains.

The Los Burros Mining District was formed in 1875 and in the first year 63 claims for gold and quicksilver mining were recorded. One mine, the "Last Chance Mine", claimed to make a profit of $200,000. But the Los Burros Mining District never produced the bonanza that was hoped for. Manchester, another boom town that developed near Jolon in the time of the gold frenzy, became a ghost town when the bubble burst. Nothing remains of Manchester today and its very location in the fastness of the Santa Lucia Mountains has been lost.

Miners at the entrance to the Last Chance Mine in the Santa Lucia mountains. (Courtesy of the Monterey County Library)

At the time of the Santa Lucia gold frenzy a

group of prominent Monterey citizens formed the San Carlos Gold Mining Company, capitalized with $50,000, to prospect for gold on Point Lobos and in the mountains nearby. But the only mineral found near Point Lobos had none of the glitter of gold.

A vein of coal discovered in the hills back from the Point led to the formation of the Carmelo Land and Coal Company in 1888. A report of 1890 showed that more than 720 feet of the mine had been timbered and that coal was to be found there in rich veins. From the mine, worked mainly by Chinese laborers, a hoisting engine brought the coal to a shute leading to the north side of Whaler's Cove, then called Carmelo Cove. There it was loaded on the waiting ship. Adverse market conditions and increased costs forced the mining operation to close in 1896.

Meanwhile maritime industries had developed in the Cove. The Carmel Company was formed in 1862

A contemporary drawing of the Carmel Company's whaling station at Point Lobos in action. (from *Marine Mammals* by Charles M. Scammon, courtesy of Robert W. Reese as used in his *A Brief History of Old Monterey*, 1969)

for whaling from the Carmel River Bay. Going out in

small boats the whale hunters cruised out as far as ten miles at sea to harpoon whales. The carcass was towed to the Cove where it was beached to be stripped of its blubber. All that remains of this today is the small whaler's cottage set back from the Cove with some of the Whale bones around it and the great iron cauldrons set in place on the shore near the entrance to the Cove.

Across the entrance to the Cove, beneath the tracks leading from the Coal Mine, an abalone cannery was set up in the early 1890's. Japanese fishermen were brought in to harvest the molluscs crowded on the rocks of the shore. When the shore had been harvested clean it was necessary to use diving suits both from the shore and from small boats to reach the

Abalone meat laid out to dry before canning, below the tracks used by the coal mining cars. Across the entrance to the cove may be seen the building of the whaling station. (Courtesy of the California Department of Parks and Recreation)

abalone. Removed from the shells the meat was laid

out on large racks before being canned. The odor of drying abalone must have filled the air around the Carmel River Bay until 1928 when the operation was discontinued.

Before the end of the nineteenth century a grid of house lots was to be marked out on the wooded land behind the Cove for the planned Point Lobos development to be known as Point Lobos City, or Carmelo. At the same time the Chinese and Mexican laborers were clearing roads for the projected 'Carmel City' on the manzanita-covered hillside on the other side of the Carmel River Bay. Both 'cities' were to go through periods of boom and bust and both were to fail. But like a phoenix from its ashes one was to rise from its failure.

Bibliographical Notes

Much useful information regarding the Carmel Valley and the South Coast is to be found in the chapters so titled in *Monterey County* by Augusta Fink (1972/78). An early publication, *History of Monterey County*, 1881, has been reprinted in a handsome fascimile edition. *Ranchos of Monterey County* by Donald M. Howard (1978) provides additional information on that subject. *Monterey Mother Lode* by Randall A. Reinstedt gives an introduction to the story of gold mining in the Santa Lucia Mountains. *Big Sur* by Toni Kay Lussier (1979) has pictures, a map and historical notes on sites in the area.

An article by Rich Wilkerson on early Post Offices in California in the September issue of *Noticias del Puerto de Monterey*, the Quarterly Bulletin issued by The Monterey History and Art Association, includes information on the first Post Offices in Carmel, Carmel Valley and the Big Sur area.

IV. Carmel City Development Fails

The rebirth of the old Carmel Mission together with the opening of the great new Del Monte Hotel on the outskirts of Monterey led to the development of a Carmel City on the Manzanite covered hill above Carmel Bay. On October 19, 1859, President James Buchanan signed a patent which confirmed the return of the Mission properties in California to the Catholic Church.

But it appered that this was too late for the Carmel Mission for in 1861 Wm. H. Brewer, a member of a geological survey party, wrote, "It is now a complete ruin, entirely desolate...Hundreds (literally) of squirrels scampered around in their holes in the old wall... about half are fallen in... the paintings and inscriptions on the walls were mostly obliterated. Cattle had free access to all parts; the broken font, finely carved stone, lay in a corner; broken columns were strewn around where the altar was; and a large owl flew frightened from its nest over the high altar."

Eighteen years later Robert Louis Stevenson was enjoying a tryst with his *inamorata*, Mrs. Fanny Osborne, among the ruins when a horrifying scream burst out overhead. Thinking of the many ghost stories told about the old Mission, the two fled in fright. When they reached the crest of the hill by the Mission they saw that the cry had come from the resident owl and not from a hidden banshee.

Stevenson had crossed the Atlantic Ocean and the great American continent to follow a married woman with whom he had fallen in love when they were both visiting France. Fanny Osbourne, who was soon to divorce her husband and marry Stevenson, was at the time staying with her sister in the old Spanish-Mexican village of Monterey. The house in which Stevenson stayed during this time is now open to tourists.

The young writer left his comments on the

Mission as he found it, "The Mission church is roofless and ruinous...As an antiquity in this new land, a quaint specimen of missionary architecure and a memorial for good deeds, it has a triple claim to preservation from all thinking people; but neglect and abuse have been its portion...The day of the Yankees has succeeded and there is no one left to care for the converted savage."

Despite the desolate appearance of the ruins and the occupation of the Mission grounds by squatters, the Carmel Mission had not been completely forgotten by the church after the act of secularization appeared to mark its demise. In the years before the U. S. government turned the property back, some occasional service of worship were conducted in the ruins for the sake of the natives who still lived in the valley.

The ruins of the Carmel Mission church in the years before the restoration began.(Courtesy of the Harry Downie Collection)

In 1880 Helen Hunt Jackson, author of the bestseller, *Ramona*, made a tour of the California Missions. Of her visit to the Carmel Mission she wrote,

"Father Junipero sleeps on the spot where he labored and died. His grave is under the ruins of the beautiful stone church of his Mission...It was perhaps the most beautiful, though perhaps not the grandest of the Mission churches; its ruins have today a charm exceeding all of the others...It is a disgrace to both the Catholic Church and the State of California that this grand old ruin, with its sacred sepulchres, should be left to crumble away."

In the same year a young David Starr Jordan, later to be the first President of stanford University, visited the area as a representative of the U. S. Census Bureau. In his report he commented, "Of all the indentures on the coast of California the most charming is the little bay of Carmelo, which lies just south of the Point of Los Pinos, between this and the rocky cape of Los Lobos." Twenty five years later he was to return to the "charming little bay" and to build his holiday house in the village that had grown by the bay.

It was in the year 1880 that the Monterey Peninsula was to take on new life. A branch line of the Southern Pacific Railroad was brought to Monterey just in time for the opening of the grand Del Monte Hotel. Built by a division of the railroad corporation it was described as "the most manificent structure of its kind on the Pacific Coast...indeed one of the largest, handsomest and most elegantly furnishd sea-side hotels in the world."

In subsequent years the ornate building was to burn down and be replaced twice. In 1943 the third hotel building and grounds were taken over by the Navy for the training of wartime recruits and in 1948 the Navy bought the complex for the present Naval Postgraduate School.

Stevenson, who was to leave Monterey after a short stay, could see nothing but disaster in that great new development which was crowding so close to the quaint adobe village of Monterey. He wrote in his farewell to the Old Pacific Capital, "The Monterey of the last year exists no longer. A huge hotel has sprung up in the desert by the railway. Three sets of diners sit down successively to table. Invaluable toilettes figure along the beach and between the liveoaks; and Monterey is advertised in the newspapers, and posted in the waiting rooms at railway stations as a resort for wealth and fashion. Alas for the little town! It is not strong enough to resist the influence of the flaunting caravanseria, and the poor, quaint, penniless native gentlemen of Monterey must perish, like a lower race, before the millionaire vulgarians of the Big Bonanza."

But the fears of Stevenson were to prove to be unfounded. The 'huge hotel' was to be instrumental in the change of Monterey from an "adobe capital of old California" to a prosperous town of new California. And the "millionaire vulgarians" who were coming to this magnificent center on the Monterey Peninsula were to prove to be the means for the rebirth of the Carmel Mission, and so one of the reasons for the coming of the village which was to grow up beside the Mission.

Fr. Angelo Delfino Casanova, for whom a street was to be named in the future village of Carmel, had taken special interest in the Carmel Mission from the time that he had come to the Monterey Parish in 1863. By 1877 he was able to reroof one room off the main church, the Sacristy, with $40.00 that he had raised for the purpose. He celebrated the mass in the roofed room on regular occasions. In 1879 he began to charge an admission fee of ten cents to view the ruins, the income to be devoted to the further restoration. In the account book that he kept he made the notation, "When this will be possible only God knows", after he had shown that the first year's receipts from the admissions amounted to $11.75.

It was with the opening of the Del Monte Hotel that his receipts began to multiply, as groups of tourists came on the Seventeen Mile Drive. The Mission ruins served as one stop on the drive and as

A view of the Monterey Peninsula as it appeared in 1880 with the railroad line from San Francisco leading by the Del Monte Station to the Monterey ternminus. The grand Del Monte Hotel is pictured in its landscapted grounds ith its race course and bath-house. The original 17 mile drive from Hotel Del Monte is seen as it passes the village of Monterey, the tent city of Pacific Grove, the Point Pinos Lighthouse and the manzanita covered hill above the carmel River Bay by the Carmel Mission near which Carmel City was to arise. (Sketch by Joe Pierre based on an illustration in *History of Monterey County*, 1881 as reprinted in a facsimile edition in 1979)

the number coming on the tallyhos from the hotel increased Casanova raised the admission price to fifteen cents. And funds for the rebuilding grew appreciably from the donations which were now being made by many of the new class of well-heeled visitors from the Del Monte holiday hotel.

By 1884 Fr. casanova was able to reroof the whole church building and to rededicate it on the one hundredth anniversary of the death of Fr. Serra, August 28, 1884. A crowd of 400 to 500 people gathered from the valley ranchos, and from Monterey and other nearby towns as well as from the hotel for the opening anew of the church that had been built in 1797. Above the rebuilt ceiling a peaked roof, in the then popular Gothic style, was raised and the assistant of the Monterey parish began to celebrate the mass at the Mission on a regular basis.

The rededication of the 1797 Carmel Mission church on August 28, 1884. (Courtesy of the Monterey Public Library)

Among those who attended the rededication were two young men who had a real estate office in Monterey, Santiago and Belisario Duckworth. Santiago at that time conceived the idea of a new Catholic Center near the Mission like the very successful Methodist retreat center at Pacific Grove, between Monterey and the manzanita covered hill above the Mission.

Belisario Duckworth caught Santiago's enthusaism for the development of such a center because this was just at the time of the land boom in California. After the completion of the transcontinental rail lines a migration from the eastern United States to California set in which was said to be as striking in some respects as that at the time of the gold rush. To handle the great influx of people new towns were being laid out on ranches and woodlands cut up into house lots.

In such a time of boom in California real estate the prospects for a residential subdivision even on a pine and manzanita covered hill looked promising. The hill overlooking the Mission, known as Rancho las Manzanitas, was used for rough pasturage by its owner, Honore Escolle. Escolle had a bakery in Monterey and for some time had been investing the profits from the bakery in land. As a rather useless bit of land for ranching the Rancho was available for development and Santiago could visualize there a city of streets filled with happy Catholics on their summer holiday.

Escolle was a hard trader and the Duckworth brothers did not have the money to buy the land. An agreement was reached by which they would pay only for the "surveying, plotting and recording of said lands" as their part of the investment in the subdivision, the profits from which were to be divided equally with Escolle. The agreement was signed on February 8, 1888, and by April of that year a survey of the property was filed with the Recorder of Monterey County. Homesites were to measure 40 by 100 feet with

A cartoon of 1888 at the time of the building of cities in the wastelands of California. As Honore Escolle and Santiago Duckworth might have looked as they were negotiating for Carmel City Sites. (From *The History of California* by A. A. Gray, 1934)

business lots 25 by 100 feet. These latter were to be on the 100 foot wide business street Ocean and "Broadway".

The enterprising young Duckworth brothers set a team of Mexican and Chinese laborers to the clearing of the pine trees and manzanita shrubs from the street lines and began to mark off the lot corners. In April of 1889 the first advertisement for CARMEL CITY appeared in the Monterey newspaper over the single name S. J. Duckworth. Santiago was going alone in the project. Promise was made in that advertisement that plans were afoot for "A Catholic Institution of Learning" in this "Catholic Summer Resort.""

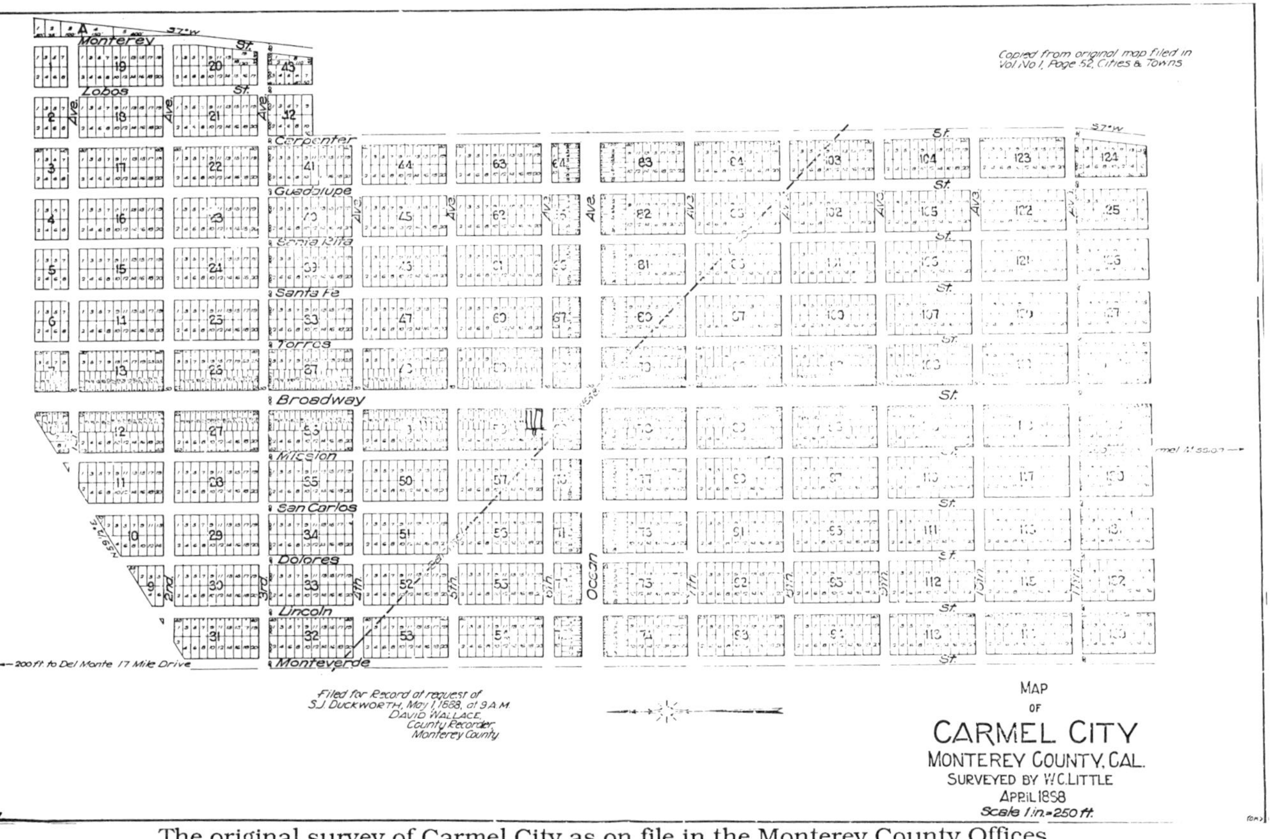

The original survey of Carmel City as on file in the Monterey County Offices.

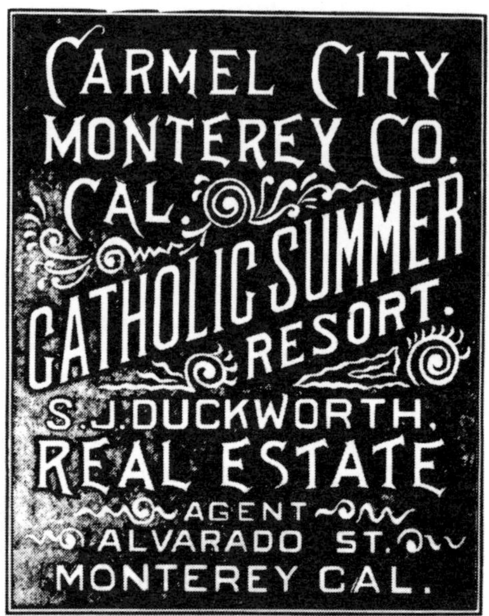

Santiago Duckworth (Courtesy of the California State Library) and cover of the first brochure of Carmel City (Courtesy of the Harrison Memorial Library of Carmel)

In the first brochure issued it was reported that seven lots were sold on the first day and that by the end of the month thirty eight lots had been purchased by future residents of Carmel City. Before the end of the year more than two hundred new owners had received deeds to resident lots in the "City". More than half of these were from San Francisco, many of them being teachers and others in the field of education who were planning vacation homes there.

The next year, 1890, was to be a very good one for Santiago Duckworth and his Carmel City project. When the young entrepeneur learned that the Directors of the Catholic Ladies Aid Society were to meet in Santa Cruz in August of that year he hurried over to present an offer to the assemblage. At that meeting he proposed to set aside five acres in Carmel

City for a park to be know as 'Paradise Park' at the corner of Carpenter and Ocean Ave. There would be constructed there an assembly hall for meetings of the catholic societies, proceeds from the sale of 100 lots to furnish the funds for the construction. After a delegation of the ladies had come to view the site they voted to accept the proposition. It appeared that the Catholic Summer Colony gave promise of becoming a huge success.

By that time some of the business men in Monterey had begun to buy blocks of lot in Carmel City for investment as had at least one enterprising business woman of San Francisco. In 1889, the year that the property was put on the market, Mrs. Abbie Jane Hunter of that city had bought seven lots in the new subdivision. Mrs. Hunter interested a group of women in the city to join her in a Womens Real Estate Investment Company for investment in Carmel City.

She brought her brother, Delos E. Goldsmith, a carpenter, with her to the new subdivision to build a summer place for her use. As the first houses in the new subdividsion he built a house for her at the northeast corner of Guadalupe St. and 4th Ave., and another across Guadalupe for her friend Miss Augusta Robinson, one of the Directors of the Womens Investment Company. These two cottages are still to be seen on the Guadalupe-4th Ave corner. The original Hunter Cottage is little changed but the Robinson cottage has been greatly altered to serve as headquarters and art gallery for the Cherry Foundation.

Delos Goldsmith opened his carpenter shop, Carmel's first business, and built several small houses on the street appropriately named Carpenter Street. These are occupied to this day. He also built for his sister a two story Hotel Carmelo in the center of the planned business district, at the corner of Ocean and "Broadway" (later to be renamed Junipero St.) There the first community event was held, a dancing party on the Fourth of July, 1891. That building was later to be moved down Ocean to the corner of Monte Verde and still exists as a part of the present Pine Inn.

The Carmelo Hotel at the corner of newly cleared Ocean and Broadway in Carmel City. The pine trees in the background were at Monte Verde Street, which marked the western limit of the original subdivision. (Courtesy of the Calif. State Library)

The disaster which was to overtake Mrs. Hunter and the Womens Real Estate Investment Company in 1895 marked the beginning of the end for Carmel City. As president of the Company Mrs. Hunter was arrested on Valentine's Day, February 14, 1895. She had to spend a day in jail as the result of a complaint that her company had obtained money under false pretenses. A woman who had purchased a lot in the Sunnyside Tract in San Francisco claimed that she had not received a deed for the lot for which she had paid.

In the same month Mrs. Hunter's mortgaged house in Carmel City was sold by the Sheriff of Monterey County when she was unable to raise the money to redeem it. The California land boom was turning to bust. The bank failures in the eastern

United Staters had begun to have an influence on California finance and so on real estate values. Santiago Duckworth was to place all the unsold lots in Carmel City in the name of his mother-in-law, Mrs. Carmen Amesti de McKinley of Monterey, and so to be out of the picture entirely.

The earlier success of Carmel City had led to a similar project across the Carmel River Bay. It appeared for a time that there would be 'twin cities' on that "most charming bay." There had been filed at the office of the Monterey County Recorder the plot of Point Lobos City, later to be known as Carmelito. Among the purchasers of lots in Point Lobos City were Fanny Osborne, later to become Mrs. Robert Louis Stevenson, and her sister, Mrs. Sanchez of Monterey.

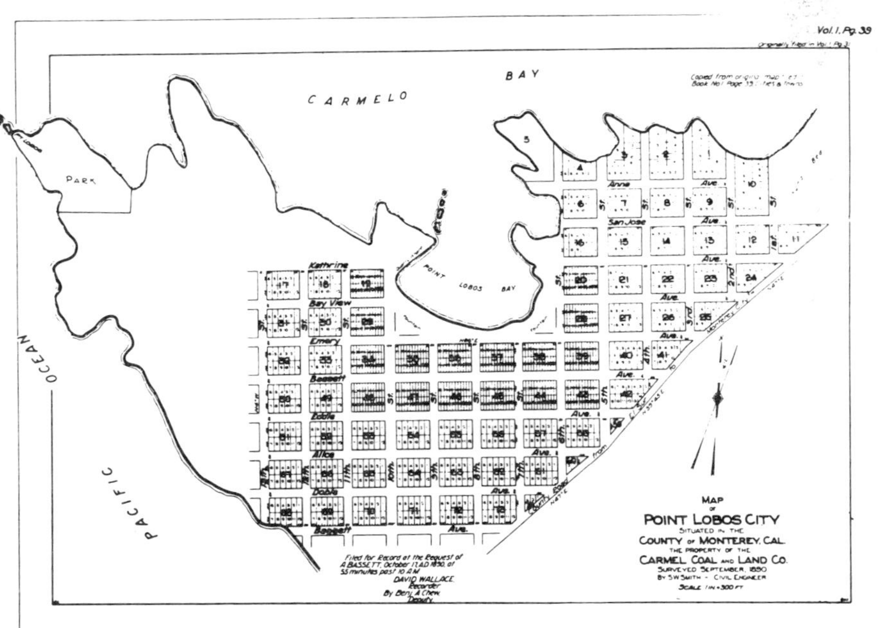

The plot plan of Point Lobos City as filed with the Monterey County Recorder. (Courtesy of the Department of Parks, State of California)

But few lots had been sold in the time of financial panic and these stood vacant when A. M. Allan of Oakland bought the 640 acres of Point Lobos from the Carmelo Land and Coal Company. He then proceeded to buy back all the sold lots from the new owners and began to prepare the Point as a retirement estate for himself.

Meanwhile, on April 18, 1895, Dr. William Saunders, a San Francisco investor, purchased 700 of the remaining lots in Carmel City from Honore Escolle. Then, five days later he bought the 89 acres of beach and sand dunes west of Monte Verde, the western limit of Carmel City, from the San Francisco and Pacific Glass Company. But he made no immediate use of these purchases, being content to hold them for better times.

Development of real estate on the Carmel Bay was at a standstill as the nineteenth century drew to a close.

Bibliographical Notes.

A good survey of the Carmel City development is to be found in an article by Elena and Elmer Logarico "Carmel's First Developers Counted on Railroad to Bring Them Riches" which appeared in the *Herald Weekend Magazine* for July 27, 1980. The chapters on Monterey, Carmel Valley and Carmel-by the Sea in Augusta Fink's *Monterey County* (1972/78) offer surveys of the histories of these regions and the facsimile edition of *History of Monterey County, 1881* (issued in 1979) is worth looking into. *Carmel-by-the-Sea in Story and Picture,* edited by Emile White (197) includes some additional information. *Point Lobos, Interpretation of a Primitive Landscape,* issued by the California State Department of Parks and Recreation (1974/75) includes a valuable chapter on "History of Point Lobos". Some copies of the weekly and daily newspapers for the years 1887 through 1901 are available on microfilm and in the original at the Monterey City Library, the Monterey County Library in Salinas, and the California State Library in Sacramento.

V. Carmel -by-the-Sea is Founded

The turn of the century marked a change in the fortunes of the Carmel project when, on November 20, 1900, Frank Powers purchased Dr. Saunders' 700 lots in the subdivision plus the 89 acres of beach and dunes that the doctor had bought five years earlier. Then, in 1901, James Franklin Devendorf, an experienced real estate promoter who had subdivisions in San Jose, Stockton, Morgan Hill and Gilroy, came into possession of the rest of the unsold lots in Carmel City.

On November 25,1902, the Carmel Development Company was formed with Frank Powers, who provided the financial backing, as President, and J. Franklin Devendorf, experienced in real estate development, as Secretary and active Manager of the enterprise. Early in the next year a map of CARMEL-BY-THE-SEA, with the name hyphenated for the first time, was filed with the County Recorder of Monterey County.

At the beginning the Carmel Development Co. sold lots with as little as $5.00 or $10.00 down payment and $5.00 monthly payments on the remaining principal. And it is reported that when purchasers fell behind on their $5.00 monthly payments it was not unusual for these payments to be allowed to accumulate for years. Good will was so important that when it was finally evident that the buyer was unable to continue his payments on a lot, the buyer was refunded all that he had paid.

A picture of Frank Devendorf and his activity in the developing Carmel-by-the-Sea resort was given by one of the first residents, "J. F. Devendorf was very active in promoting the sale of lots, flying around in his horse and buggy through the bushes and over the logs at an amazing rate. No high powered sales tactics were used. The person had to have the desire to purchase a lot and Mr. Devendorf would simply aid him to select one that he liked.

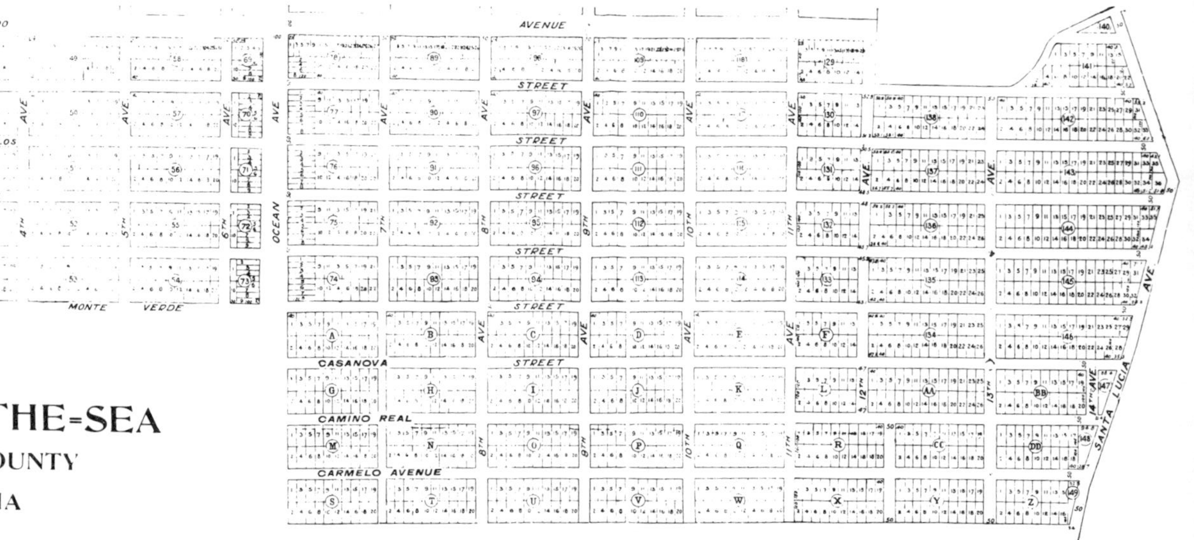

The plot plan that was included in the first sales brochure showing that the main interest was in selling lots west of Junipero Avenue. The enlarged area west of Monte Verde and south of 12th Avenue extended the bounderies (Courtesy of the Harrison Memorial Library of Carmel)

J. Franklin Devendorf, developer of the Carmel-by-the-Sea subdivision, admiring one of the native pine tress that he valued so highly. (Courtesy of the Hathaway Collection).

He was most solicitous for the comfort of those who located here and was called upon to attend to all sorts of commissions, from getting a tube of burnt sienna for Miss. e. Chandler to assisting one of the Murphys across the Ocean Avenue when it was like a river during a downpour. He also provided water for the people when the pump broke down. He was called the father of Carmel."

Frank Powers, President of the Carmel Development Company, holding his grandaughter, Mrs. Wm. E. Fassett of Nepenthe in Big Sur. (Courtesy of Mrs. Fassett)

Frank Powers remained generally as a silent but very active partner in The Carmel Development Company. It was he who chose the names for the new streets in the enlarged area west of Monte Verde. The first street to the west was named for Fr. Casanova, the first restorer of the Carmel Mission. The third new street was to be named San Antonio, for the Mission in the Santa Lucia Mountains founded by Fr. Serra next after the Carmel Mission, and the last street by the beach was to be called Scenic Road, but neither of these appeared on the first sales brochure plot.

Jane Gallatin Powers, Mrs. Frank Powers, was an accomplished artist who often entertained well-known artists at the Powers home, 'The Dunes', to conduct classes in the garden by the sea. She was to be instrumental in forming the Carmel Art Association which today has its beautiful permanent gallery on Dolores Street. That Carmel-by-the-Sea was to become an artist colony was largely due to Mrs. Powers and her associates.

It was on May 21st, 1903 that J. F. Devendorf, as Manager of the Carmel Development Co. sent out a circular letter addressed "To the School Teachers of California and other Brain Workers at in-door employment", The letter read:

"The town of Carmel-by-the-Sea offers special inducements to you for 1903 since heretofore it has been kept from the notice of the public because of lack of good roads. The 17 mile drive touched it to the north, and went back to Monterey, and the County road skirted it on two sides and came up behind it on the sough at the Carmel Mission. Neither road passes through it.

"Now the Carmel Development Co. have (sic) built a first class easy graded road from Monterey Railway Station, which is only three miles away, directly to the beach of Carmel-by-the-Sea.

"We have acquired a whole mile of beach and all the land fronting on it.

"California is growing so rapidly, that the time has come when the promotors of new towns can determine the general character of the residents. We want brain-workers, because they enjoy the picturesque scenery and need a climate for a vacation place so equable that they can be out-doors the whole day long.

"We have arranged for a general store, for a

butcher, for a baker, and all the necessaries of life. We have piped the town for water, and have arrangements for water the same as Pacific Grove and Monterey. All the necessaries of life are made convenient.

"All we need is population.

"We have determined to induce the increase of population for the year 1903 without thought of profit. For that reason we intend to run the Hotel, tents and Boarding Houses at practical cost, so as to induce people to come to see our property and make them satisfied, in hope of selling them lots.

"There will be no place in California that will furnish first-class home comforts at so small a price as will the Hotel and Boarding cottages at Carmel-by-the-Sea.

"Special rates to clubs of ten.

"For particulars, address,
"J. F. DEVENDORF,
"Mgr. Carmel Development Co., Monterey, Cal.,
"or 330 Pine St., San Francisco, Cal."

The letter had the desired effect and school teachers as well as college professors formed the nucleus of the early summer residents of the developing colony to the south of San Francisco. Dr. David Starr Jordan, who had discovered the "most charming little bay of Carmelo" in 1880 bought three lots at the corner of Camino Real and 7th Avenue in December of 1904. The $1,500 house built by Jordan, the Preseident of the young Stanford University, must have appeared to be a mansion among the $500 cottages that the other college professors and teachers were now erecting as holiday cabins. Along Camino Real a 'Professor's Row' was soon to develop in the first block south of Ocean Avenue. The seaside resort came to be equally attractive to the faculty members of the University of California whose cabins were scattered throughout the subdivision.

In 1903, the year that the promotion letter had

been sent out, the Hotel Carmelo had been lifted from its foundations at the corner of Junipero, moved to the middle of Ocean Ave, set on rollers and pulled down the street by a team of mules. The old building was then incorporated into a larger structure at the corner of Ocean and Monte Verde and renamed the Pine Inn. So many people were attracted to the new subdivision that the hotel had to set up tents on the grounds for the overflow guests.

When the new Pine Inn was ready for its grand opening on July 4, 1903, Carmel's first restaurant opened on the corner of Ocean and Dolores. Mr. and Mrs. Melvin Norton, who owned a grocery store in Pacific Grove, erected there a tent on a 20 by 30 foot floor provided by Devendorf. Adjoining the restaurant tent a frame hut had been built for the kitchen while other tents were set up as quarters for the proprietors and their employees.

Camping out on Ocean Avenue in Carmel-by-the-Sea. (Courtesy of the Monterey County Library)

Up Ocean Avenue, at the corner of San Carlos, an old lady had pitched her tent, outside of which she set up a kitchen stove with a tall chimney, a rack for her pots and pans and a stand to hold her parrot in its cage. She proved Devendorf's claim that Carmel's climate made it possible to be "outdoors the whole day long." One early resident said that in the early days "Providing of food was simple. If we decided to have rabbits we just took our shotguns and went around the corner on Lincoln and bagged a few...The rubbish situation was also very simple. A pile of waste paper was placed in the center of Ocean Avenue and burned."

There was just one store in Carmel-by-the-Sea in 1903, the company store opened by the carmel Development Company for the convenience of the new residents. One of the summer visitors the next year was Louis S. Slevin, who was to begin the building up of the business district. After enjoying the 40 cent dinner at the Pine Inn he was so impressed with the possibilities of the new resort that he purchased a business lot on Ocean Ave. at the prevailing price of $325. After the lot was cleared of pine trees a store building was erected for him..

Slevin opened a stationary store in the new building and applied for the Carmel Post Office permit. Until then the 'Carmel Post Office' that had been opened in 1893, was far up the valley, near the present Carmel Valley Village. It had been placed there for the convenience of the valley ranchers and the few residents of Carmel City received their mail through the Monterey Post Office, as being more convenient than the P. O. located far up the valley.

Remembering the opening of that Post Office in Carmel-by-the-Sea, Slevin wrote years later regarding his first decision as the Postmaster, "As soon as the post office started a representative of a lock box manufacturer came down from San francisco to try to sell me boxes. I found that the fewest that could be bought was a row of eight and I told him that was ridiculous - we'd never need so many." He admitted "my estimate was incorrect" for he noted that in 1945 the Carmel Post Office boasted 1,955 boxes..

The Louis Slevin Stationary Store on Ocean Ave. with Carmel's post office. (Courtesy of the Monterey County Library)

Today there are 5,086 boxes in the Carmel-by-the-Sea Post Office with the zip code 93921, and another 1,500 boxes in the 'Carmel' Post Office at the entrance to the valley with space for 1,000 more, using the zip code 93922. There is, moreover, R.F. D. delivery from that office to 5,000 recipients outside the incorporated limits of the town, with the zip code 93923. And the Carmel Valley P. O. has 1,000 boxes with an R.F.D. delivery list of about 1,300 with the zip code 93924.

Before the local post office was opened mail was brought from Monterey and distributed at the company store. When the post office opened in Slevin's store the daily gathering simply moved to that location. There has never been house-to-house mail delivery in the incorporated town of Carmel-by-the-Sea because the town fathers refused to install sidewalks and to issue house numbers. It is said that the refusal to make provisions for such house delivery of mail was based on the desire to continue the daily 'post office gathering' which is continued to this day.

Shwenigen's Bakery on the South side of Ocean between Dolores and Lincoln was built just two lots away from Slevin's store soon after that was opened. The Carmel Bakery is located there today. (Photograph by Margeurite Temple)

One building is still to be seen on Ocean Avenue that was in the original group. Shwenigen's Bakery was built just two lots away from Slevin's store and the building with its prominent bay windows still stands and holds a bakery. Within a short time a butcher shop and plumber had joined Slevin's store and bakery on Ocean Avenue. The supplies for the stores were sent by sailing vessel from San Francisco to Monterey and hauled over the hill.

The watering trough at Ocean and San Carlos which once offended the developers of Carmel when large icicles gathered there after a very unusual spell of freezing weather. (Courtesy of the Harrison Memorial Library of Carmel)

A rather elaborate watering tough with a tile roof was built at the corner of San Carlos and Ocean which was a boon to the settlement in which horse power was figured literally. It presented a problem, however, for the developers of the town on one unusually cold morning when the temperature dropped below freezing, as it seldom does in Carmel. The water dripping from the roof formed long icicles as a result of the unusual weather. Slevin rememberd that "when Mr. Devendorf saw these he became very excited at such possible detriment to the sale of lots. He promptly had the offending intruders knocked off and buried."

At this time each neighborhood had a stand for the delivery of milk, known among the natives as "milk shrines". They were divided into compartments which bore the name of the patrons and every morning Mr. Waterbury, the milkman, would drive in from the valley with his horses and wagon and deposit the full milk bottles in the proper sections. Old timers remember that an abandoned "shrine" stood on Carmelo near Ocean until 1931.

A carmel 'milk shrine' loaded with the day's supply. Courtesy of the Monterey County Library)

Early street signs were carved to represent the name of the street, Ocean Avenue had a sign carved with waves, while Mountain View showed a scene of mountains and trees. The Livery Stable at Ocean and Mountain View is shown in the background of an early photograph of the street sign at that corner.

The original street sign at the corner of Ocean and Mountain View with the Livery Stable in the background. (Courtesy of the Monterey County Library)

Water was a cause for concern in the early days. At first water was supplied by the pipe line from up the valley that had been built to supply water for the great Del Monte Hotel and grounds. But after a few years the Carmel Development Co. had decided to put in its own system. A pump was installed at the river and water piped into a large tank at the corner of Ocean and Mountain View. Water for those living higher on the hill was carried in a horse-drawn barrel on wheels.

That water problem intruded into one of the 4th of July parades as an early resident remembered, "The porch at Pine Inn was crowded with guests eagerly waiting for the parade to pass. In due time it came along and at the end of it the large barrel on wheels with a sign on it, 'Carmel Reservoir'. A high official who was present saw no humor in the idea and waved his arms in fury and shouted, 'I won't have my parade insulted. I can lick my weight in wild cats, etc., etc.' But after games and races on the beach the day ended peacefully".

Rain water presented a problem in winter because the original Carmel City plan had caused the streets to be laid out running straight down the hill to the sea. In order to break up this free flow of water, which cut gullies in the newly cleared lots prepared for construction of cabins, the Development Co. put about fifty Japanese workmen to planting thousands of young pine trees. Incoming residents were encouraged to plant trees, furnished by the Company, on their land.

The forested look of Carmel-by-the-Sea results from the fact that the manzanita covered hills and sand dunes were planted with pine trees early in the century through the foresight of Frank Devendorf and his associate Frank Powers. The natural apearance has been so carefully safeguarded that to this day streets must give way to pine trees. A street will curve one way or another to miss a tree or divide, leaving the tree in the middle of the road. The pine tree symbol painted on the posts at the street corners might well be considered as memorials to those far-seeing pioneer developers.

The row of pine trees planted along each side of Ocean Ave. by the old wooden sidewalks have not been completely lost as they stand today between cement walks and curbs. And the little trees planted by the Carmel Development Co. in the middle of the 100 ft. wide street designed for Carmel City are now the giants that give the shopping area a large part of its charm. Indeed the whole of the village of Carmel-by-the-Sea retains the look of a forest because those elected to guide the town's destinies since incorporation have been just as careful to preserve its trees as were those who started the development of the town at the beginning of this century.

Trees planted along Ocean Avenue in the growing business area. Selvin's Store and Post Office, Schweniger's Bakery and the town's first Grocery Store are to be seen on the south side of the street. (Courtesy of the Bancroft Library)

At the end of Ocean Avenue there was a bath house where a towel and dressing room could be had for 25 cents. There was a 'life line' which ran out into the sea for about 100 feet, supported by floats placed every few feet. At the end of the rope there was anchored a small raft for the use of the swimmers hardy enough to swim in the frigid waters.

The Bathhouse served as a social center in the early days and Carmel's first social club, appropriately called "The Manzanita Club", was organized there by Thomas Burnright, the first Bathhouse manager. This was a men's club that continued to be active for many years and was later to build its own clubhouse in the center of the town. The Bathhouse was sold in 1929 to

Mrs. W. C. Mann who tore down the building in order to use the material to build a dwelling for herself. A depression was to be seen in the sand for many years where the Bathhouse stood and even today storms and strong winds will sometimes lay bare the remains of the foundation beams.

The Carmel Bath House on the beach at the foot of Ocean Avenue, which was the center of much Carmel social activity for many years. (Courtesy The Monterey County Library)

In the summer of 1905 the Arts and Crafts Club began its meetings in the Bathhouse with Miss Eliza J. Allen, an early Carmel artist, as president. Mrs. Powers, a leader of the artists in Carmel from the beginning, was elected vice-president while Louis Slevin served as treasurer. By 1907 this club had built a clubhouse on Monte Verde at a cost of $2,500, money raised from art fairs and other benefits. The Carmel Art Association began as a chapter of the Arts and Crafts Club.

In 1910 The Carmel Development Company donated land on Mountain Ave. for the Forest Theatre and paid for the first seats and stage on the cleared ground. Set in a glen in the forest with a stage placed within a natural growth of pines, benches were arranged on the hillside. Early publicity read, "The local literary folk co-operate in producing plays on the open-air stage annually...On account of the peculiarities of the stage setting, the character of the plays is necessarily unique and the interest of the whole colony in the enterprise is so great that its success as an incentive for further literary productions of a dramatic character is assured."

The original logo of the Forest Theatre as reproduced in *Carmel at Work and Play* as published in 1925. (Courtesy of Lacy Williams Faia)

There was such a demand for new houses in the summer colony that Devendorf ordered some old San Francisco cottages dismantled and shipped down in pieces to be reassembled in Carmel. It is reported that when the first ship arrived it contained parts of one cottage, parts of a barn or two and a great mass of doors. Materials for building were so scarce and the demand for houses so great after the cottage and barns had been rebuilt on newly purchased lots, some people took the doors and constructed simple cottages from them. An example of such a door-house may still be seen in the front half of the little yellow house set down low on the west side of Lincoln between 9th and 10th. This example of an early summer cabin, as

The "house made of doors' which still stands on the west side of Lincoln between 9th and 10th. (Photograph by Marguerite Temple)

preserved in only the front half of the present cottage, shows what the first holiday houses were like in Carmel-by-the-Sea. The narrow 40 foot lots limited the size of the cabins and the imagination of the owners, who were usually their own builders and architects, gave the variety which Carmel Cottages still show. Every time one walks down a street in town another 'gem' is discovered which was missed on the last stroll.

Transportation to and from Carmel was a problem that had to be solved. There were, of course, no licenses of any sort and anyone with a team and wagon could provide service. Wesley Hunter began to take ladies to Monterey in his buckboard for a day's shopping in the Carmel City development and and continued his service after Carmel-by-the-Sea was established. The expedition took up the greater part of the day, from early morning until well into the afternoon. Later the 'Carmel bus' was the standard form of transport from the Monterey railroad station to the Carmel hotels. On that trip the driver would stop when he got halfway up the Carmel Hill, telling all male passengers that they must get down to lighten the load and walk up the hill. The Carmel Hill continued to be

The horse drawn 'bus' for the Monterey Railway Station in front of the Hotel Carmel. (Courtesey of the Harrison Memorial Library of Carmel)

a stiff grade until it was cut down for the new highway in 1929. It was said that the first low powered motor buses had to back up the hill, while the horse stages could make the pull forward.

Carmel's first school was financed by the Carmel Development Company because there were not enough students to qualify for county assistance. The seven children who were in town in 1904 met with their teacher, Miss Mary Westfall, in the former carpenter shop of Delos Goldsmith on Dolores. By 1906 a public School had been established and a two room building had been built for it on the northest corner of San Carlos and 9th. In this mission style building with its false bell tower 48 pupils met with Miss Westfall and the second teacher, Mr. Saxe. With additions made during the years that followed that was the Sunset School which was in existence in that location until 1965 when new schools were built elsewhere in the community and the building in that place became the Sunset Cultural Center.

A library was started in 1904 by Mrs. Helen Jaquith in her cottage. She sought to add to the collection of books by giving the right to borrow books to any who would contribute a book. On October 5, 1905 a group was gathered together by Frank Powers contributing one dollar per year as dues. It was not until 1908 that the first library building, given by the Carmel Development Company, was opened at the corner of Lincoln and 6th with Miss Hoyt as Librarian.

Beginning in July, 1911 the brochures of the Carmel development appeared quarterly as the *Carmel-by-the-Sea Courier.* In a 1913 issue there were pictured the new public buildings on which the community prided itself. The new Public School, the Public Library, the Arts and Crafts Club building and the Forest Theatre were pictured as well as the town's churches, the Carmel Mission, the Methodist Church built in Mission style, the Presbyterian Chapel and All Saints Chapel of the Episcopal Church.

In that issue there was a plot plan which showed the golf course laid out on what was then known as Mission Point and is now simply called "the Point." In time the golf course was to be divided into more lots for the subdivision but the golf hut still stands at the northeast corner of San Antonio and 14th, enlarged to serve as a private home.

By 1913 there were about 550 year round residents in Carmel-by-the-Sea by the milkman's census, with several thousand vacation residents joining these in the summer months. Many of the shops in the growing business district on Ocean Avenue were only open for the summer season.

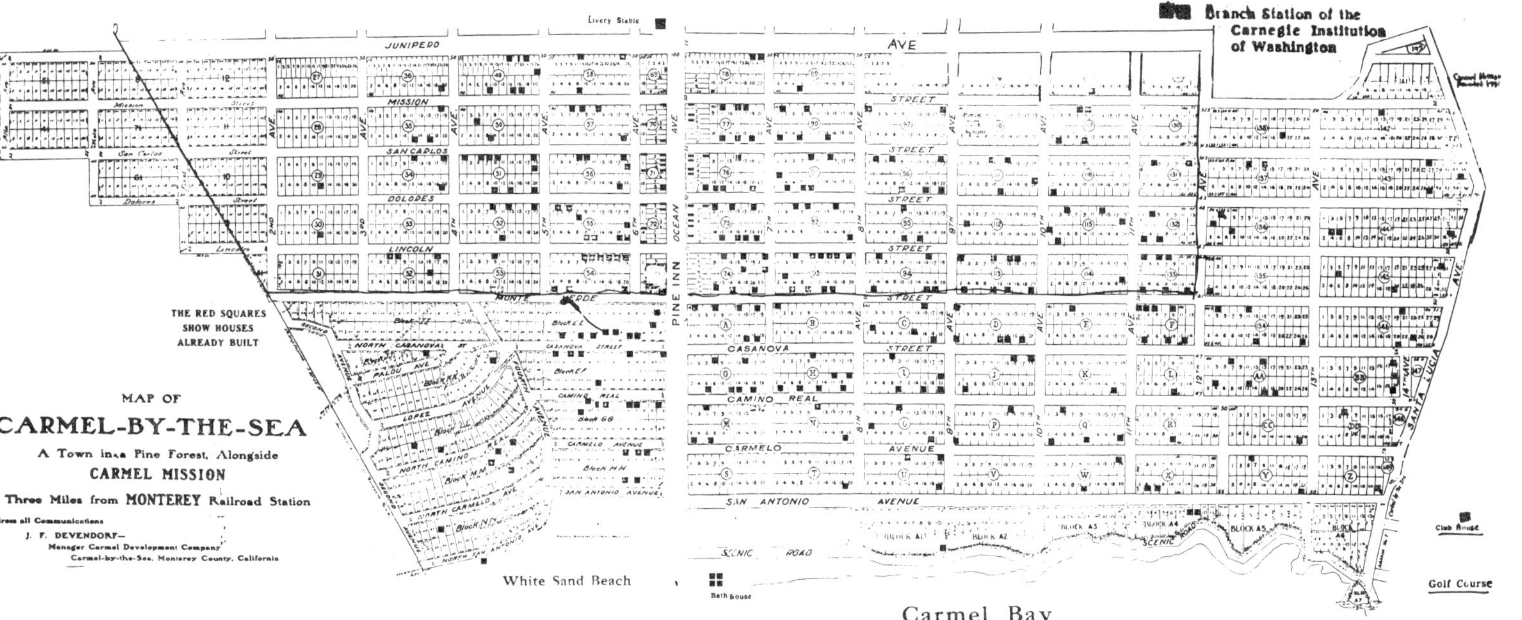

The plot plan as printed in the 1913 brochure with black squares showing where houses had been built by that time. (Courtesy of the Harrison Memorial Library of Carmel)

The plot plan of that year is of special interest because every house built west of Junipero were marked. This map, described CARMEL-BY-THE-SEA as "A Town in a Pine Forest alongside CARMEL MISSION, three miles from MONTEREY presented by J. F. Devendorf, Manager Carmel Development Company." It is most appropriate that the park in the heart of town, at Ocean and Junipero, should carry the name of the man who richly deserves the title, "Father of Carmel."

Bibliographical Notes

Material on the history of Carmel in the period from 1902 to 1913 is to be found in the Historical Collection of the Harrison Memorial Library in Carmel. It includes copies of brochures issued by the Carmel development Co. in those years as well as articles from the period, or written later about the period. More historical material of this sort is to be found in the Monterey City Library, the Monterey County Library in Salinas, the California State Library in Sacremento and the Bancroft Library at the University of Califormia, Berkeley.

The story of the first Carmel Post Office is told in an article "Early Post Offices in California" by Rick Williams in two 1968 issues of *Noticias del Puerto de Monterey*, the quarterly bulletin of the Monterey History and Art Association. A recent work by a long-time resident of Carmel, Sharon Lee Hale, under the title *A Tribute to Yesterday* (Valley Press, Santa Cruz) is of great value in the emphasis that it puts upon the people who have settled and lived in Carmel, individuals and families.

Photographs of the artists, Jane Gallatin Powers and Sydney Yard, together with brief remarks concerning each, are to be found in *Yesterday's Artists on the Monterey Peninsula* by Helen Spangenberg (1976)

VI. A Bohemia-by-the-Sea Develops

At about the time that Devendorf was sending out his circular letter to the 'indoor brain workers' that resulted in the development of Professors Row, Frank Powers was describing the glories of the seaside resort to George Sterling, a budding poet who worked in San Francisco and lived in Piedmont across the bay. As a leading attorney of the city Powers was a member of the Bohemian Club as was Sterling, the poet. This contact was to have a strong influence on Carmel development for it was around the house that Sterling was to build there that a 'Bohemia-by-the-Sea' was to be formed in the next score of years.

That side of Carmel's development, which was never reported in promotional brochures, was given full publicity in an article that appered in the *Los Angeles Times* on May 22, 1910. The article was by Willard Huntington Wright, the Literary Editor of the *Times* who was later to be the editor of the magazine, *Smart Set* and was to write stories about Philo Vance, the detective, under the name S. S. Van Dyne. Headlined, HOTBED OF SOULFUL CULTURE, VORTEX OF EROTIC ERUDITION, the article promised to tell of "Carmel in California, where author and artist folk are establishing the most amazing colony on earth."

Commenting that "The Carmelites include a great many well-known writers and artists as well as many artist and writers who hope to be well-known", Wright introduced the leading figures of the bohemian community: "It is here that Jack London creates his red-blooded yarns...Alice MacGowan and Grace MacGowan-Cooke, consanguinary and literary sisters, hold forth at Carmel and write best sellers...In Carmel lives the wassail bard, George Sterling. But Sterling is not a real poet, his sense of humor is too keen and he is too interested in life...At Carmel lives James Hopper, a favorite with the magazine readers...Mary Austin is a revelling center of temperament. Temperament exudes from her and stands around her like an aural integument..."

"It is at Carmel", he continued, "that Upton Sinclair holds forth and shakes the foundations of the universe with his feverish novels...From San Francisco comes Xavier Martinez, the painter, whose features can only be seen at close range...To Carmel came Arnold Genthe, San Francisco's society photographer, the esthete of the camera, the ne plus ultra of the off-focus portrait... Then at Carmel are Fred Bechdolt, writer of short stories (Upton Sinclairs's right hand dietitian) and Ina Colbrith, the poet...Chris Jorgensen has a large house at Carmel; Jorgensen is a rapid-fire society artist...Ferdinand Burgdorff is another painter who has a cottage in Carmel; he has a fine termperament in embryo which at present is still mere peevishness, but it is developing rapidly...Herbert Heron is the esthete of Carmel; an unappreciated poet who writes long iambic pentameter affairs concerning Actaeon and kindred personages...But I cannot tabulate any more. Life is short and the list of Carmelian artist is long."

George Sterling, the acknowledged leader of the pack of bohemians in the new Carmel development, had begun to write his poetry on the ferry ride from Piedmont to San Francisco. He had been encouraged in his writing by Ambrose Bierce, Literary Editor of the *San Francisco Examiner.* When the first small editon of his poems, *The Testimony of the Sun,* was brought out, Bierce made the extravagant prediction, "You shall be the poet of the skies, the prophet of the suns."

At this time another budding writer, Mary Austin, was staying with the writer, Herman Whitaker, and his family in Oakland. Earning her living as a teacher in the Owens Valley, she had come to the Bay area in connection with stories that she was selling to *The Overland Monthly,* a San Francisco magazine. Whitaker had been impressed with the sensative style and penetrating observations which so caught the

Gathered on the porch of the Sterling house were four aspiring authors, Jimmy Hopper, Fred Bechdolt, George Sterling and Herman Sheffauer. (From *The Seacoast of Bohemia* by Franklin Walker)

spirit of the desert land and people that he found in *The Land of Little Rain,* Mary Austin's first published book.

When George took Mary to lunch at Coppa's Restaurant, the meeting place of the San Francisco Bohemians, she told him of her desire to visit the Carmel Mission where she had planned to lay some of the scenes of the novel *Isidro* which she was then writing. Mary's intention to make a visit to the Carmel Mission gave George just the push that he needed for he couldn't get Carmel out of his mind since his talk with Frank Powers. Plans were made then and there for the trip to the new resort of Carmel-by-the-Sea via the train to Monterey. When they saw the little houses built on the tree-covered hillsides overlooking the blue waters of the little bay each decided that this would be the perfect place to settle for the pursuit of literary activities.

George was first to make the move. Planning to finance his venture by some part-time work in his uncle's real estate office in the city, he took his wife, Carrie, to Carmel and began to build his house on Torres Street in the largely undeveloped southeast section of the village.

Sterling discovered that the Carmel climate was so mild that even in midwinter he could sit naked on his porch, "with a dressing gown at hand" he explained, "lest a wandering spinster notch the enjoyment". As Wright had written of his life in Carmel, "Like Yates at Innesfree, Sterling has nine rows of beans. he raises potatoes and catches his own fish. He lives the life of an outdoor Indian. He is happily married, unlike many of the Carmelites and when he writes it is for his own amusement." Carrie found housekeeping in Carmel was reduced to a minimum, though there were new problems such as the skunk who wandered into the house.

Mary Austin soon followed the Sterlings to Carmel. Using money saved from her meagre salary as a teacher and the little that she was now realizing from her writing, she had a small house built on Monte Verde from which she had a sweeping view of the bay. Working on a writing platform that she had built high in the pine trees on her property she completed the novel, *Isidro*, with its scenes at the Carmel Mission. It was said that Mary's writing platform was second only to the mission as a tourist attraction at that time.

Mary was soon to be known for her eccentricity as she walked the woods or the beach with what were described as 'flowing Grecian robes", her abundant gold-brown hair loose over her shoulders or braided Indian fashion. The flowing robes may well have been adopted to hide her stocky figure but they served to add to her reputation as an eccentric.

Jimmy Hopper followed soon after Sterling and

Mary Austin's writing platform from which she looked to the open sea. (From *The Seacoast of Bohemia* by Franklin Walker)

Austin had settled in Carmel, bringing his wife to a house near the beach which they rented for $6.00 a month. He hoped that the stories that he was beginning to sell to magazines would provide frugal support - and if things became too bad he knew that he could borrow from his friend, George. Things did often get bad and when he did go to his friend for a loan, that friend would, in turn, borrow some more from his uncle in San Francisco who was having a great success in his real estate business there.

Hopper had been an outstanding football player at the University of California, being one of the trio that first stole the Stanford Axe, the symbol held each year by the winner of the intercollegiate 'Big Game'. After his graduation in 1898 he had gone through the Hastings Law School and passed the state bar examination but had never practiced law. Instead he had worked as a reporter on the *San Francisco*

Jimmy Hopper and Mary Austin on Austin's writing platform as she points to the view of Point Lobos across the Carmel river Bay. (Courtesy of the Harrison Memorial Library of Carmel)

Chronicle, been on the staff of *The Wave,* a literary weekly and had taught school in the Philippines for two years. He returned to Oakland to write stories of his Philippine adventures for *Sunset* and other magazines.

After Jack London and his wife came to Carmel to visit the Sterlings in their newly built house he related his impressions of Carmel and some of his experiences there, put into fictional form, in his novel, *The Valley of the Moon.* In that novel a couple from Oakland, Billy and Saxon, who resembled Jack and his wife Charmaine, leave the city to find the perfect place for their permanent home. Though Carmel was not the place finally chosen it was certainly under consideration----five long chapters of the book are devoted to the experiences of Billy and Saxon in the village and surrounding area which are evidently Carmel and the surrounding Big Sur region.

Sterling, Austin, London and Hooper on the Carmel beach. (From *Earth Horizon*, the autobiography of Mary Austin)

Of the reaction of the Carmel 'crowd' to London, Mary Austin wrote that some could not take seriously his "recent discovery of Darwinian Evolution" but that the bohemians were more receptive to his Marxian Socialism: "We were not, at Carmel, inclined to the intellectual outlook, except that there was a general disposition to take Jack seriously in respect to the Social Revolution." He who had a rubber, stamp, "Yours for the Revolution, Jack London" to go above his signature on letters, was made to feel at home by the bohemians of Carmel.

Many writers and artists came to Carmel after the San Francisco earthquake and fire of 1906. The loss of so many old buildings in the city meant the loss of the cheaper quarters, causing the writers and artists to seek the less expensive and readily accessible housing in the resort village to the south. One who was later to be a popular member of Carmel's bohemian colony had an unforgettable first-hand experience of the earthquake. Xavier Martinez, an artist of Indian ancestry, had come from Guadalajara Mexico to study at the Mark Hopkins Art School. After going to Paris for further study he returned to set up his studio in the Latin Quarter of the city where he had studied.

When his San Francisco studio was destroyed he was taken in by Herma Whitaker in Oakland, where he soon married Whitaker's daughter, Elsie. In her reminiscences, recorded sixty years later for the University of California, Elsie told the story of the night of destruction as she had heard her husband tell it:

"At about 4 A. M. on April 18th Xavier returned to his studio in the Montgery Block after a meeting of the Bohemian Club and an extra hour of conversation accompanied by the imbibing of a considerable quantity of *Vino* at Coppa's Restaurant in the same building. By the time he reached his studio he was wide awake and sat down at his desk to sketch out the next day's work.

"Suddenly the Michelangelo cast on the top of the bookcase shot into the middle of the room shattering it and his mirror on casters (for his models) whirled around in a mad dance. Then, when his chair began to bounce, he muttered 'I can't be as drunk as that' but the familiar sounds of crunching and cracking of separating brick walls recalled the earthquakes of his youth in Mexico. Instinctively he shot into the entrance alcove, a safety measure in Mexico where the arches were protection from falling timbers.

"A bit shaken and with much trepidation he watched the wall over his bed open up and with a tremendous crash fall into the alley below. A gentle dawn, hovering over the sleepless city, shed its soft light into the studio and over the tons of bricks resting on his bed. Marty stepped outside to find the landscape changed. The Italian quarter was almost flat and Chinatown was mostly in ruins."

Elsie and Martinez in Carmel with Herman Whitaker, her father. (Courtesy of the Monterey County Library)

A few years later the couple began coming to the Del Monte Hotel in the summers where Xavier gave courses in Rollo Peter's Art Gallery in the hotel. Soon they began to move to Carmel in the summer where he taught classes for the Arts and Crafts Club.

A considerable group was to come to Carmel from the community of writers that had been formed by Upton Sinclair in Englewood, New Jersey, across the Hudson from New York City. In the winter of 1906 Sinclair had established the community, known as Helicon Hall, with the $3,000 in royalties that he had received from his book, *The Jungle*, an expose of the Chicago stockyards. That experimental colony which was characterized in the newspapers as a 'hotbed of radicalism and free love' was destined to be in existence for only one winter for on a very cold night in March 1907, the building burned. One drunken carpenter, who may have inadvertently set the fire, lost his life while the writers lost their life's collection of notes and manuscripts.

Among the writers in that community who would later make Carmel their headquarters were the writers Alice MacGowan and her divorced sister, Grace McGowan Cooke along with Upton Sinclair himself. Though Sinclair appeared to have been inspired by his walks in the hills and forests and along the Carmel beach, he was never completely 'at home' in Carmel. Some of those wedded to the free bohemian life of the artistic community found him, as Carrie Sterling wrote in her diary, "too egocentric and a zealot in urging in others his ideas as a 'perfid teetotaler' and nonsmoker."

Another alumnus of Helicon Hall to come to Carmel in that period was Sinclair 'Hal' Lewis. Hal, as he was called, perhaps to save confusion with the other Sinclair, had dropped out of Yale before completing his course in order to try his new life as a writer. After the fire he had returned to Yale to complete his course. When Grace MacGown Cooke wired him to come out as the part-time secretary for the sisters, he came at once in order to be near to Helen Cooke, the oldest daughter. But Helen was never attracted to Lewis whom her sister described as "fresh, gifted, pimpled and generally disliked."

Some eleven years before Lewis was to have his marked success in his book, *Main Street*, a visitor to Carmel was impressed by his fund of stories. William

Rose Benet remembered one experience as he related, "On the way home from George Sterling's, through the Carmel woods, of a summer night, he would launch into some yarn that he had made up on the spur of the moment - and before we were back at our cottage the whole story would have been completed in recitative. It was a marvelous performance and apparently his fund of invention was inexhaustible."

The group of writers often joined for picnics on the Carmel beach or on Point Lobos. At these picnics the Abalone was the central feature. In his book about his Carmel experiences London wrote of a beach picnic when he first heard 'The Abalone Song'. With the fictional Mark Hall representing George Sterling, London wrote, "Now listen, I'm going to teach you all something, Hall commanded, a large rock poised in his hand above the abalone meat. You must never, never pound an abalone without singing this song. Nor must you sing this song at any other time."

"At the wave of his hand other poised stones of the Tribe of Abalone Eaters came down in unison on the white meat and the voices were uplifted in the Song to the Abalone. Old verses all sang, occasionally someone sang a fresh verse alone, whereupon it was repeated in chorus...And so it went, verses old and new, verses without end, all in glorification of the succulent shellfish, of Carmel."

Remembered as among the original verses composed by Sterling were:

Oh some think the Lord is fat
And some think that he is boney,
But as for me I think that he
Is like an abalone.

Oh some drink champagne,
And whiskey by the pony
But I will try a dash of rye
And a hunk of abalone.

Oh some like ham and some like jam,
And some like macaroni,
But our tom-cat live on fat
And juicy abalone.

Jack London's own verse, as found in his book, was

The more we take, the more they make,
In deep-sea matrimony.
Race suicide will ne'er betide
The fertile abalone.

There never was any shortage of the abalone which were to be pried off all the exposed rocks around the bay. It is said that one one memorable day Sterling and Hopper harvested fifty-five sacks of the large shellfish in a few hours. It may be that the story was enlarged in the telling but there is no doubt about the plentitude of the abalone at that time. The tough abalone meat cannot be cooked and eaten until it is throughly beaten. The abalone song made a game of this necessary activity.

It was Jimmy Hopper's widow. Elayne, who copied down the score for the song many years later:

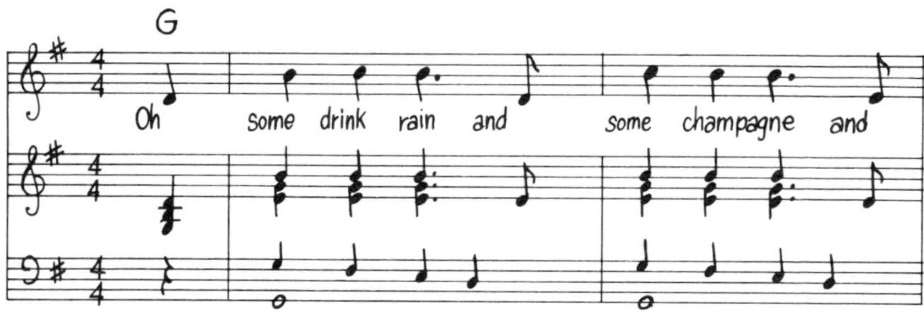

The writer and artists of the bohemian community entered whole-heartedly in all the community activities of the Carmelites. One of the most popular annual affairs was the 'International Dutch Fair' held to raise money for the building of the Arts and Crafts Clubhouse. Each year tables and counters were set up among the pines in the small park that was across Ocean Avenue from the Pine Inn. Carrie Sterling was in charge of the Dutch booth with other ladies of the village presiding at the French, Spanish, Italian, Scotch, Irish and Japanese booths plus the Colonial Booth to represent the United States.

The affair was opened with a parade down Ocean Avenue being led by a 'Dutch Band" which no person from Holland would ever recognize as such. The members of the band wore burlesque costumes and played instruments not usually found in a marching band, from a banjo to an accordian. This was the men's part of the activity generally, though one year Sinclair

A picnic of the 'Bohemian crowd' of Carmel at Carmel Point Beach as Elsie 'Pelly' Martinez would remember it. (cartoon by Joe Pierre)

Mrs. E. J. foster, Mrs. Carrie Sterling and Mrs. Connolly in costume at the Dutch Booth of the International Dutch Market. (Courtesy of the Harrison Memorial Library of Carmel)

'Hal' Lewis acted as the Master of Ceremonies for the whole day, dressed in the outfit of a Dutch Matron.

Van Wyck Brooks was one among many who were to find Carmel a romantic setting for nuptials, coming to the resort in 1911 for his marriage in the Mission Church. Though he was to visit here often after taking up his position on the faculty of Stanford, he did not find that this was a place conducive to creative activity. In his *Scenes and Portraits* he wrote that "Carmel was wildwood with an operatic setting where life itself also seemed operatic and where curious dramas were taking place in the bungalows and cabins, smothered in the blossoming vines on the sylvan slopes..."

"The writers there gave themselves over to day-

Sinclair 'Hal' Lewis in his costume as Master of Ceremonies at the International Dutch Market. (Courtesy of Monterey County Library)

dreams while their minds ran down like clocks as if they had lost the key to wind them up with, and they turned into beachcombers, listlessly reading books they had read ten times before and searching the rocks for abalone. For this Arcadia lay, one felt, outside the world in which thought evolves and which came to seem insubstantial in the sunny air."

Whether Brooks' evaluation of the decline in

literary activity was warranted or not, things were certainly beginning to break up in this Bohemia-by-the-Sea. Hopper was spending more time in New York than in Carmel as he hawked his stories to the New York publishers. Mary Austin went to Europe where she was lionized by the literary lights of England. And when she returned in 1914 it was to find that a winter storm had wrecked her tree-top writing platform and that the bohemian element in the town was in a turmoil.

Alice MacGowan had quarrelled with her sister and had moved out of their house into a shack of her own. Arnold Genthe's fame as a photographer had so increased that he closed his Carmel studio and moved permanently to San Francisco. Chris Jorgensen had moved from his stone house after the death of his wife and it had become a boarding house that was eventually to become the La Playa Hotel.

George Sterling was having an affair with Vera Connally, a young woman who had recently come into the village. Soon Carrie left George to return to Peidmont to live with her sister who had married George's uncle. George's latest affair was just one too many for Carrie and her sister was urging her to divorce him.

George moved out of his house because the big room where so many parties had been held was too full of memories for him. Moving into a cabin on his land he asked his friends John and Ethel Turner "to live in the house, cook for him and hush the demanding voices of his memories." After a time Carrie returned to try to make a go of the marriage again. In his diary George wrote, "It's grand to have Carrie back! She's on a grand cleaning orgy now and will probably lose ten lbs. before she's done."

But his joy was to be shortlived. The last entry in his diary was made on November 24, 1913, "Carrie has left me to sleep at Hoppers tonight and go to Berkeley on the morning bus." The reconciliation had not worked and three weeks later Carrie filed for divorce on the grounds of her husband's constant drunkenness and failure of support. After the divorce was granted George left Carmel for New york where he tried to find a new life among the bohemians of Greenwich village.

After an unhappy year in New York Sterling returned to San Francisco, taking up residence in the Bohemian Club. Because his uncle had lost most of his wealth in Real Estate investments, an anonymous friend paid for his room and keep at the Bohemian Club for the rest of his life. For the next decade George was what one boigrapher has called, "the heart and ruler of San Francisco Bohemia...to California and above all to San francisco, The Poet." As an official Poet Laureate of the city he was chosen to write the Ode to the Panama Pacific Exposition.

Jack London's suicide at the Glen Ellen Ranch was a great blow to Sterling. A contemporary remembered his visits to the ranch "with its innocently rowdy parties where people laughed and sang and played practical jokes and where Sterling could give vent to the sharp wit which is the obverse aspect of all his deep melancholy." The main ranch house had burned and some of London's prize horses had been poisoned. London had fallen out with the local leaders of the Socialist Party and he blamed the members of the party for these troubles. On November 22, 1916 he took a dose of poison which may have been one of the phials that had been distributed to members of the Carmel bohemian community by Carlton Bierce who, it was said, got his supply through his position in the San Francisco Post Office.

Sterling was in New York conferring with his publishers when the next suicide came as a tremendous shock. Two years after London's suicide, Carrie took the same way out of her troubles. Elsie Martinez remembered the occasion, "After two years Carrie finally decided that she could not adjust herself to the dull single life of a divorcee. She missed the gay, colorful life in Carmel, the swarm of visitors in their house there and sharing the honors with her poet. She realized that she had made a mistake and that there was nothing to do but take the suicide route...She had put on the beautiful dressing gown over a lovely filmy nightgown, arranged her hair elaborately and on a little record machine beside her bed put on Chopin's *Funeral March.* Then she took the drink from her vial of cianide and passed away before the record stopped."

George lived on in the Bohemian Club for another eight years but never really got over grief for Carrie's death. It was H. L. Menken who, on a visit to the Bohemian Club on November 16, 1926, discovered that Sterling had committed suicide in his rooms. It was reported that the immediate cause involved Menken's visit. George had looked forward to the visit of his old friend and while waiting for his arrival from Los Angeles had consoled himself with several bottles of wine.

Menkin's arrival had been delayed for several days and when he did arrive George was too intoxicated to serve as the toastmaster at the club dinner. A writer whom George did not like had taken Sterling's place as toastmaster and when Menken finally came to George's room after the dinner he found him dead with cianide poisoning. Menken, who left San Francisco before the funeral, was said to have remarked coldly, "Sterling was wise to bump off. Booze had him and he was impotent...He was 57, old enough to die."

Mary Austin never really settled again in Carmel after she returned to find the storm destruction. She was to find a new 'soul home' in the desert country of New Mexico. In 1919 she began to work with the School of American Research in Sante Fe and in 1925 built her *Casa Querida*, 'House Beloved', there. Three years before that she co-authored a book, *Taos Pueblo*, with one who was to be one of Carmel's most noted residents in later years. Mary wrote the text to go with the photographs of twenty-five year old Ansel Adams who in his latter years settled south of Carmel where he took an active part in the decisions regarding the future of the Big Sur area before his death on April 22, 1984.

One member of Carmel's bohemian period lived into the 1980's. Elsie Whitaker Martinez spent many summers in the village when "Marty" was teaching art in the Arts and Crafts Club summer program. Both she and her husband were active members of the community of artists and writers before the first world war. She subsequently moved to Carmel where she celebrated her 90th birthday in the Carmel Boy Scout Building on the first of march, 1980, surrounded by a host of her Peidmont and Carmel friends.

Elsie Whitaker Martinez, Marty's 'Pelly', at the age of 90 sits in her Carmel home, formerly the studio of Xavier Martinez, remembering Carmel's colorful past. (Courtesy of the *Monterey Peninsula Herald*, photograph by Ben Lyon).

The reminiscences of 'Pelly', the nickname given her by Marty by which she was known to all, recorded her reminiscences of the bohemian days for the Oral History Series of the Bancroft Library of the University of California. Those reminiscences, published as a book titled *Elsie Whitaker Martinez* in 1969 by the University of California give the only first-hand report of the people and events of Carmel in the pre-war period.

Bibliographical Notes

The primary source book for this chapter is the book of recollections, titled *Elsie Whitaker Martinez* (1969) in the San Francisco Writers and Artists series of the Regional Oral History Office of the Bancroft Library, the University of California, Berkeley. A fine book on this period, now out of print, is *The Seacoast of Bohemia* (1966/73) by Franklin Walker, late Professor of English Literature at Mills College. Franklin Walker was one of those who interviewed Elsie Martinex for the aforementioned book.

Sketches of the life of George Sterling are to be found in *They Were San Franciscans* (1941) by Miriam Allen De Ford, in which chapter XII is titled, "Laureate of Bohemia, George Sterling," and in *Tales of San Francisco* (1957/62) by Samuel Dickson, chapter XVII, A recent complete biography is *George Sterling,* 1869-1926 by Thomas E. Benedikston, which was published in 1980.

Mary Austin wrote of her own life in *Earth Horizon, Autobiography* (1932). Other works on her life and work include *Mary Austin, Woman of Genius,* by Helen Knight Doyle (1965) and *Mary Hunter Austin* by T. M. Pierce (1965). *Room and Time Enough, The land of Mary Austin* (1979) is a recent 'coffee table book' with an interesting collection of selections from Austin's writings illustrated with photographs by Morley Baer, and an introductory biographical sketch by Augusta Fink, and in 1983 there was published Miss Fink's full biography of Mary Austin, titled *I, Mary.*

Enlightenening articles on the bohemian period that have appeared in the *Weekend Magazine* of Monterey's *Sunday Peninsula Herald* include: "Pelly Martinez' Bohemian World" by Bonnie Gartshore in September 15, 1974 issue, and by Elena Logario the three articles, "Pied Pipers of the Arts; The Three Pied Pipers of Carmel, Sterling, Genthe, Austin Brought Arts to the Colony for the November 12, 1978 issue, "Ode to a Succulent Mollusc, The Peninsula's Folksong in Praise of the Abalone" for April 27, 1980, and "Coppana Made his Restaurant in San Francisco Colorful

Headquarters for Bohemian Hijinks" for April 19, 1981.

A brief survey of the life and work of Xavier Martinez, together with a color illustration of his painting 'Monterey Landscape' are to be found in *Yesterday's Artists on the Monterey Peninsula* (1976) by Helen Spangenberg, and a catalogue of the Xavier Martinez works in the Oakland Museum of Art (1974/82) by George W. Neubert is available at the museum. Similar brief surveys of the life and work of Chris Jorgensen and Charles Rollo Peters are to be found in the book by Helen Spangenberg, as well as notes on the other Carmel artists, Jane Gallatin Powers and Sydney Yard.

VII. Incorporation as a City in First War Years

Preliminary steps were taken in 1916 for the incorporation of Carmel-by-the-Sea as a California city. Many townspeople were opposed to the move for fear that this would change the character of the tranquil artist colony that had grown up by the sea. Mass meetings were held to oppose the move and arguments for and against the move appeared in Carmel's weekly newspaper, *The Pine Cone* which had been founded the year before by William D. Overstreet as Editor and Publisher.

The *Pine Cone* had appeared as a result of a push from the south of the state. As Overstreet wrote, "One day there came a rumor that a Los Angeles man was planning to start a newspaper here. The following week the *Pine Cone* was born." Though the paper has passed through many owners and editors it continues as the voice and record of the town. In the very first issue one of the long running conflicts of the twonspeople was seen in a filler urging 'Pave Ocean Avenue'. That hope was not to be fulfilled for another seven years as the members of the artistic and scholastic summer colony feared that 'outsiders' would flood the town if the main street was paved.

Nevertheless the necessary applications for incorporation were made in August of that year when the total population of the town numbered 600. On November 1 a vote was taken on the question with the result that 113 voted for incorporation and 88 opposed it, On January 1, 1917, Carmel-by-the-Sea became an incorporated city under california law.

J. E. Nichols was elected City Clerk and the pioneer storekeeper of Carmel, L. S. Slevin, the City Treasurer. The city Clerk served as Assessor as well as Tax Collector and in the January 31 issue of *The Pine Cone* some 500 of the citizens were listed as being delinquent in their taxes. Three and a half pages of the paper were taken up with this list of overdue assessments, from 97 cents to $5.26.

In addition to the City Clerk the only salaried officer of the new 'city' allowed by the incorporation order was the Town Marshal. 'Gus' Augustus Englund was appointed to this position and he was a familiar figure for many years as he patrolled the streets as Carmel's only peace officer on his horse, 'Billy'.

The Town Marshall "Gus" Englund on his horse "Billy", Carmel's complete police force for many years . (Courtesy of the Monterey County Library)

The lead article in the *Pine Cone* for April 14, 1915, was headlined, "Carmel Must Have Fire Protection". In that article it was stated that "No property owner can afford to refuse a contribution to this most necessary object." The response was encouraging for in the next week's issue it was announced that C. D. Goold had offered his garage to hold the fire extinguisher vehicle and to pay half of the cost. Carmel's Fire Department was well on the way to permanent establishment when at a mass meeting a film of the great fire at Ocean Park, California, was shown and an additional $200 was collected.

Carmel's chimney sweep provided the earliest fire prevention for homeowners. (Courtesy of the Monterey County Library)

The need for adequate fire protection was brought home to Carmelites when the Pebble Beach Lodge was completely destroyed by fire on December 27, 1917 with the loss estimated at $50,000. Pebble Beach was at that time considered to be a part of the Carmel region for the masthead of *The Pine Cone* read, "Devoted to the interests of Carmel-by-the-Sea, Pebble Beach, Carmel Highlands, Carmel Valley."

The Carmel Fire Department which had been under county rule was, on December 20, 1917, made a municipal organization with D. W. W. Johnson as Commissioner of Fire and Police. Plans were made at that time to build a firehouse to the rear of the building in which the city offices were housed.

Carmel's first movie theatre was set up in the oldest building in the village. What had been a barn on

An early picture of the Carmel Highlands, Carmel-by-the-Sea, Monterey Stage at the Carmel Stage headquarters, over which were the first offices of the city of Carmel-by-the-Sea. (Courtesy of *The Carmel Pine Cone*)

the Rancho Manzanita of Honore Escolle had been taken over as the clubhouse for the men's club, The Manzanita Club, and there the 'Manzanita Picture Theatre' was established. Admission prices were 20 cents for adults, 10 cents for children. Charles D. Curtis, an ex-prizefighter, was projectionist and general factotum for the films shown there.

On the days that films were to be shown in the evening Curtis would drive his cart, drawn by 'Peanuts', through the village streets with the sign "Movie Tonight" displayed on the back. In the evening he would sell tickets and popcorn to those beginning to assemble until he felt that there were enough of an audience for the showing of the film. Then he repaired to the back of the room where he hand cranked the projection machine. The piano accompaniment for the film was provided by Saidee Van Bower.

Charles D. Curtis, projectionist and general factotum for the movies shown at the Manzanita Theatre drawn up in front of the hall in his pony cart. (Courtesy of the Monterey County Library)

At the declaration of war by the United States patriotism flared in Carmel as it did in the rest of the country with the entry into the European war. Ninety young men registered for conscription in Carmel on May 31, 1917, a day that was marked by patriotic speeches and a parade down Ocean Avenue.

War news filled the pages of *The Pine Cone* for the next few years. Accompanying an article of April 11, 1918, "What About the Boys Who are Fighting for You in france" there was a cartoon appeal from the Red Cross entitled, "The call from No Man's Land." The

American Red Cross had come to Carmel before the U. S. entry into the war, the local chapter having received its charter on October 23, 1916. From its present local headquarters on the corner of Dolores and Eighth Avenue, the Carmel Red Cross chapter provides 24 hour service for local emergencies and is the center in town for the blood donor services.

The problems on the home front were represented by the articles on the food shortages. "California Faces Sugar Famine, Individual Saving Will Prevent It" was a headline on August 1, 1918. An article on "New Wheat Rules for Households" of September 12 was accompanied by a statemnt by Dr. Roy Lyman Wilbur of Stanford University titled "Fighting With Food." In this period *The Pine Cone* carried a series of cartoons by Robert True to condemn 'food slackers'.

The widening influenza epidemic was reflected in the articles in the local paper as the war drew to a close. "Uncle Sam's advice on Flu" was followed by one headlined "U. S. Health Service Issues Warning" in which it was stated that "Influenza is expected to lurk for months." And influenza was not the only health problem. On August 28, 1919 there was news that William T. Kibber, the health officer of the city, warned that everyone should be vaccinated for smallpox because there had been several cases in the county near Carmel's borders.

Carmel had a double celebration at war's end. Due to a rumor that went around the country the first celebration came several days before the officeial end of the war at 11 o'clock on the 11th of November, 1918. Of the town's celebrations an article in *The Pine Cone* for November 14 read, in part, "What if Carmel was a little previous last Thursday in celebrating the victorious peace. At least we had an opportunity to give vent to long pent-up emotions. And we were not alone; New York, Chicago, San Francisco and other cities fell for the same fake news.

The Call From No Man's Land

An appeal for the support of the Red Cross as it appeared in *The Carmel Pine Cone* for April 11, 1918. (Courtesy of the Harrison Memorial Library of Carmel)

Swatting the Food Slacker

Everett True, noted patriot, joins United States Food Administration in drive on conservation shirkers

A cartoon condemning the 'food slackers'. (Courtesy of the Harrison Memorial Library of Carmel)

"When the honest-to-goodness news came on Monday we had a big bonfire celebration on Ocean Avenue. Bob Leidig sent up patriotic baloons. We all sang 'The Star Spangled Banner' and 'God Save The King'.. Then we heard a plea for Carmel people to do their allotted share in this week's United War Fund Campaign. After that, young folks and old danced on San Carlos Highway."

Carmel celebrates the World War I victory with a patriotic parade. (Courtesy of the Harrison Memorial Library of Carmel)

The world war was over but a 'war of words' continued unabated in Carmel. The condition of the street was the bone of contention and the paving of Ocean Avenue the bone being tossed around. Elsie Martinez recalls that when she came to Carmel in 1915 with Marty, when he was teaching at the Summer Art School, their car stuck in the sand up to the hub caps on Ocean Avenue. Another recalled, in a letter written to *The Pine Cone* , that the main street of the town was "a dusty road full of holes ruts and gullies" and that "the principal bumps were known by name - the devil's staircase, the witches caldron, the hinges of hell, and others." In one of the many articles in the paper urging the paving of the street it was stated that "When heavy rains washed out gullies four or five feet deep they were filled with bushes from nearby lots. A number of persons who liked this type of art protested at paving Ocean Avenue."

A contemporary cartoon gives an idea of Carmel in the days of road paving. (Courtesy of the Monterey City Library)

Indeed it was the members of the artistic and literary community who led the protest against the paving. One letter to the paper which expressed their point of view read in part, "We do not believe that a roadway of 'asphalt macadam' would be desirable for Carmel at any price...the charm of Carmel is its village paths and roads. The curbs, culverts and other 'city fixins' would not only be out of place in Carmel but would put us in the class with Pacific Grove."

The opponents had won the first skirmish in

1919 when bonds for the cost of the paving of Ocean Avenue were defeated for the majority in favor fell short of the percentage needed to carry a bond proposition. Then in 1921 when the supervisors did pass the proposition which called for the paving of Ocean Avenue the group opposed to paving brought action in court to stop the action.

Ocean Avenue as still unpaved in 1921. (Courtesy of the Monterey County Library)

Finally, in 1922, the main street of Carmel received its pavement. A cement road was build on each side of central parkway on Ocean Avenue from Junipero to Monte Verde. This arrangement, which makes for the beauty of the shopping street today, was possible because the original developers of "Carmel City" in 1886 had laid out 100 foot wide streets for the town center -Ocean Avenue running east and west and Junipero (then called Broadway) to run north and south.

Pines had been planted along each side of the street as well as in the central parkway. Why there are no trees on the north side of the street was explained in a letter to *The Pine Cone* which read in part, "A prominent contractor who engaged in paving Ocean Avenue, knowing how the people loved their trees and not daring to touch them by day, came at night and removed every tree on the north side of the street for considerable distance, and when the business people arrived for work the next morning, there wsn't a tree, nor a hole in the ground, not a chip to tell the infamous tale. Great indignation was expressed but nothing could be done about it. All the anger in the world could not put back a single growing thing. We Carmel people love our trees. It is in our blood."

Carmel now has one of the strictest laws of any town in the country protecting its trees, none of which may be cut without the permission of the town authorities. And when side streets all over town came to be paved, trees were left in the middle of the road with the street dividing around each, The pine tree symbol is to be seen today on each of the posts which mark the street corners in the town.

Newly paved Ocean Avenue as it appeared in 1922. (Courtesy of the Hathaway Collection)

It was in 1921 that the Carmel Country Club was organized. Fred Bechdolt, the writer, and Edward Kuster, who was soon to build the first Golden Bough Theatre on Ocean Avenue, were among the directors. Great plans were made for the club which was to occupy six lots on Junipero at Ocean Ave. Included in the plans were a fine clubhouse with two tennis courts adjoining as well as a handball court and a 'clock golf' layout. Without a full golf course the club failed and the site is now occupied by the Carmel Presbyterian Church.

The area to the south of Santa Lucia which had been a golf course at one time and a small airfield at another became the the field of play for the twice-weekly softball baseball game of the Abalone League. The teams were made up of players of all ages, some whole familes and some families with players on opposing teams. Among those remembered as having played in the league were the writers Jimmy Hopper, Harry Leon Wilson, and Byington Ford as well as Bob Stanton the architect and Sam Morse, the developer of Pebble Beach.

The baseball field at Carmel Point with a game of the Abalone Softball League in progress. (Courtesy of the Harrison Memorial Library of Carmel)

It is said that the Abalone League was the first softball league to request a ruling on a disputed play from Judge H. K. M. Landis, the Commissioner of Baseball. As the first organized baseball league in the western states it served as the center for Carmel social life as well as its athletic activities. Among the dozen teams in the league were the Shamrocks, the Reds, Giants, Pilots, Robins, Sox, Rangers, Crescents, Eskimos and Sharks. The league continued to be active with the diamond located in different places in the village until 1938 with a short revival in 1947.

The Pilots, one of the dozen teams in the Abalone League. Back row, L. to R., Jack Eaton, Byron Pryor, Vic Renslow, partly hidden by the clerk of the La Playa Hotel (whose name is forgotten), then Waldo Hicks, Martin de Amaral, Raoul Root and Ruel King. Seated in front were Jessie Leslie and Mildred Farrel. (Courtesy of Mr. Waldo Hicks)

The old golf course, air field and baseball field at 'The Point' south of Santa Lucia was subdivided as 'The Walker Tract' by Mrs. Willis Walker who bought the land from the Stewart Ranch. With lots the same small size as those offered by the Carmel Development Company within the village limits, the new development had curving streets unlike the grid pattern of the original layout of Carmel-by-the-Sea and some street lights.

In 1922 a $15,000 bond issue was passed by the town voters to buy the sand dunes at the end of Ocean Avenue. Before that the villagers had no legal entry to the beach. After that vote the Carmel Development Company gave the remainder of the beach front to the city of Carmel-by-the-Sea by Deed of Gift. This meant that the city owned all its beach frontage for the first time. The beach beyond the village limits was later to be purchased by the State Park Commission so that the frontage on Carmel Bay is to be forever available for public use.

A view of Scenic Road when Carmel Point was first subdivided, with the site of Tor House atop the hill. (Courtesy of Donnan and Garth Jeffers collection)

A new street, called Scenic Road, was then built in the arid land by the dunes. On this road Robinson Jeffers, Carmel's most famous poet, was to build his Tor House and Hawk Tower. This is now owned by the Robinson Jeffers Tor House Foundation and is open to visitors at certain times of the week.

A memorial to the men of Carmel who gave their lives in the First World War, then called The Great War, was erected in the middle of Ocean Avenue at the intersection of San Carlos, site of the old town watering trough. At the dedication a parade led by Jo Mora included the Eleventh Cavalry Band of the Monterey Presidio followed by "school children, service men, citizens on foot and in automobiles" according to the newspaper report.

The dedication of the War Memorial on Ocean Avenue at San Carlos Street in 1922. (Courtesy of the Hathaway Collection)

Marching down the northern side of the double avenue from Junipero to Monte Verde, the procession turned and countermarched up the south side to San Carlos. There the parade halted at the western end of the central parkway for the conerstone laying of the 17 foot high drinking fountain designed by C. Sumner Greene.

The drinking fountain at the site of the original watering trough is now gone for when the memorial was remodelled in 1979 this was omitted from the middle of what had become a busy street and an unsafe place to stop for a drink of water. It was at that time that the memorial to Carmel citizens killed in the Second World War was set up in Devendorf Park at the corner of Ocean and Junipero.

Bibliographical Notes

A longer version of this history of Carmel-by-the-Sea by Sydney Temple is available in typescript for reference at the Harrison Memorial Library of Carmel under the title *Carmel-by-the-Sea, A Unique California Community.*

The only other source for information regarding the history of Carmel in the years covered in this chapter is the file of copies of *The Carmel Pine Cone* . A complete file of back issues is kept in the offices of the*Pine Cone* at the corner of Ocean Avenue and San Carlos. There is also a complete set of filmstrips covering the issues of the paper in Carmel's Harrison Memorial Library which are available to any who would wish to see them .

VIII. The Towering Poet of Carmel

On December 13, 1916, a poem by J. Robinson Jeffers appeared in the *Literary Digest.* And in the same year several of his poems were included in the annual *Anthology of Magazine Verse* and in the *Yearbook of American Poetry* . It was predicted therein that "California is now to have its part in the poetry revival. Robinson Jeffers is a new poet, a man whose name is yet unknown, but whose work is of such outstanding character that once he is read he is sure to be accepted."

John Robinson Jeffers and his wife Una had come to Carmel from Los Angeles in 1914 when Carmel's time as a 'Bohemia-by-the-Sea' was beginning to draw to an end. As if it were an omen of the passing of the torch from the bohemian group of writers to Carmel's new poet, who was to become world famous, Robin and Una happened on the deserted grove behind the George Sterling house soon after their arrival in the village.

In the next few years Sterling was to visit the Jeffers often in the Tor House which they were to build by the sea. And Sterling produced the first book of many that were to be written of the life and artistry on carmel's most famous poet, *Robinson Jeffers, The Man and the Artist* (1926)

The Tor House of Una and Robin was the first house to be built on the newly laid out Scenic Road. Carmel's pioneer builder, M. J. Murphy, was engaged to construct on the hill above the new road a stone house modelled after a Tudor barn that Una had admired during her stay in England. Una called the place 'Tor', an Anglo-Saxon word for the outcropping of rocks upon a hill.

The house was built of stones brought up from the shore below in a horse-drawn cart. Jeffers hired himself out for $4 a day as an assistant to Murphy's master mason both to keep down costs and to provide an outlet for his excess energy. By the time that the family, Robin and their twin boys, moved into their new home Robin was an accomplished mason.

In the years that followed Jeffers was to spend his mornings at his desk in the bedroom under the eaves of the stone house, struggling to bring forth the lines that were to make him one of America's most controversial poets. His afternoons were spent in struggling to bring stones from the beach below his property and to construct a stone garage by the house.

Jeffers laying stones for the foundation of a building on the Tor. (Courtesy of the Donnan and Garth Jeffrey Collection)

Aware of her husband's continuing need for physical activity to balance the struggle involved in his creative writing, Una asked that he undertake the major task of building a stone tower by the stone house. It may well be that the inspiration for this tower came from Una's memory of the tower of the ruined Norman castle, Thor Ballylee, in County Galway, Ireland, that she had seen while waiting for her divorce from Edward Kuster so that she could marry

Robinson. Whatever the model, this tower building project came at just the right time in the poet's life. The building of the tower in the afternoons paralleled the growth of his poetic store. As he lifted the stones into place he was planning the verses that he would be writing the next morning.

For the lower levels he rolled the stones up a long inclined ramp like those the Egyptians are said to have used in the building of the pyramids. As the tower grew, Jeffers rigged up a pulley system with which he hoisted the boulders into place. When his stone work was completed he spent his afternoons planting cyprus and eucalyprus trees on the barren hillside above Scenic Road. His son reported that he planted two thousand trees in all, making a small forest around the stone buildings. In later years, most of the land in Robin's grove of trees was subdivided and sold as small lots from which many of the trees were cut to make room for the houses. A sample of the original grove remains on the corner lot which adjoins the Tor House property.

Tor House and the tower under construction as seen from Scenic Road. (Photo by Una's Kodak, Courtesy of the Donnan and Garth Jeffers Collection)

Inspired by his surrounding and supported by his family, Robinson Jeffers was finding strength in the writing of a new sort of poetry. Around his experiences along the shore and in the mountain valleys that he and Una explored around Carmel and Big Sur he built narrative poems which were to be such a shock to readers that no publisher would touch them at first. Those were the poems destined to make his reputation as one of America's leading poets.

Soon after he and Una moved to Carmel in 1916, Macmillan had published a collection of Jeffers early love poems under the title *Californians.* But after they had settled in Tor House he became discontent with this earlier work. As he told of his decision to change his style of writing:

"The sea-fog was coming up the ravine, fingering through the pines., the air smelled of the sea and pine-resin and yerba buena. My girl and my dog were with me. And I was standing there like a poor God-forsaken man-of-letters, making my final decision not to become 'modern'. I did not want to become slight and fantastic, abstract and unintelligible. I was doomed to go on imitating dead men, unless some impossible wind should blow me emotions or ideas, or point of view, or even rythms, that had not occurred to them."

The 'impossible winds' did begin to blow as he was building what he was to call "Hawk Tower." In those years he was to find what a biographer was to call his "strange and violent voice" in which he was certainly to imitate no dead men. In explanation of his poetry he was to write of himself in the third person:

"Jeffers takes the unhuman outer world for his reality, of which human spirit is a phantasmal and transient by-product. The people in his verses have to act and suffer as intensely as possible in order to show at all against the magnificense he feels in the world outside them. He thinks the human spirit can find its peace by realizing its unimportance, and its value by realizing the beauty of the outer world."

When he sent a group of his poems, written in this new mood, to Macmillan publishers they were turned down "as lacking the grace and charm of his earlier work." Though the publisher's reply stated that "genius is evident throughout the work both of style and philosophy", such kind words availed nothing. Next, Una dispatched a packet of her husbands' poems to New York in the hands of Jimmy Hopper, the story writer. Though Hopper was well known by the leading publishers there, he was met by nothing but rejections in his attempt to market Robinson's work.

Determined that his new poems should be seen by the public Jeffers decided to 'prime the pump' by printing a book of poems at his own expense. He had published some of his earlier poems in 1912 without success, under the title *Flagons and Apples.* Of the 500 copies printed twenty were kept by Jeffers and the balance sold to a second hand bookstore for twenty cents each. So it took some courage and great confidence for the unknown poet to act as as his own publisher again.

Of this experience he later wrote: "I saw a little advertisement by a New York printer, Peter G. Boyle, in the book-review section of the *New York Times* . . . The advertisement offered printing, not publishing, and my mind reverted to my folly of 1912, yet with differences. This time I had no extra money burning my pocket; on the other hand, it seemed to me that the verses were not merely negligible, like to old ones, but had some singularity." He commissioned Boyle to print 500 copies of *Tamar and Other Poems.*

In the narrative poem *Tamar*, which was representative of his new work, he certainly offered somthing which had 'some singularity'. In that, destined to be one of his most famous poems, he harked back to the text of the Old Testament, in which he had been so thoroughly grounded by his father years before. The brief account of the rape of David's daughter, Tamar, by her brother Amon, he

Robinson Jeffers standing in the doorway of Hawk Tower. The initials U R J cut into the headstone stand for Una, Robin Jeffers. (Courtesy of the Pat Hathaway Collection)

remembered from the 13th chapter of the second book of Samuel.

Taking nothing but the name Tamar and the event of rape from the biblical story, Jeffers reversed the roles and created a Greek type of tragedy built on incest and guilt. This he set in the burned out cabin that he and Una had seen by the Mal Paso (Bad

Passage) Creek just inland from Point Lobos. The story of the poem was suggested by the rumors about those who had lived there, perhaps as they had been embroidered by Una's telling.

But this new excursion into self-publishing was again to be a disappointment. After some review copies had been distributed by the printer with no favorable reactions, 450 copies were sent to Carmel in a large packing case that was to be stored under the eaves of Tor House for many years.

Undefeated, he proceeded to send copies to persons who might appreciate his work, including James Rorty and Mark Van doren. His choices proved to be most advantageous for Rorty reviewed the poem *Tamar* in the *New York Herald Tribune* and Van Doren gave it favorable notice in *The Nation.* On the strength of those reviews interest in the new poetry of Robinson Jeffers was aroused and a New York publisher, Bone and Liveright, became interested.

In 1925 they brought out the title *Roan Stallion, Tamar, and Other Poem by Robinson Jeffers.* And in quick succession came his new works, *The Woman at Point Sur (1927), Cawdor (1928), Dear Judas (1929) and Descent to the Dead (1931).* These were the most fruitful years for Jeffers who now had an enthusiastic publisher and a growing group of readers. In England the Hogarth Press, the London publishing house of Virginia Wolfe and her husband, brought out editions of *Cawdor* and *Dear Judas.*

As his fame spread honors came to him. He received the Book of the Month Poetry award in 1937. Honorary degrees from his alma maters, Occidental College and the University of Southern California followed and he was made an honorary member of the literary honor society, Phi Beta Kappa, at its headquarters at the College of William and Mary.

In 1940 he was chosen to inauguarate a Poetry Series at the Library of Congress and on the trip to the East and back he lectured at Harvard, Columbia and at the University of New York, as well as at the state universities of New York, Kansas and Utah.

His greatest success, which was to spread his reputation far and wide, was to come from his translation of the Greek Play *Media* in 1945. Judith Anderson, already a well known actress, had come to Carmel in 1941 to take the part of Clytemnestra in the Forest Theatre productions of Jeffers' "The Tower Beyond Tragedy" a long poem in dramatic form based on a work by the Greek poet Aeschylus.

On July 4, 1941 the first performance of the "Tower. . ." was presented in the theatre among the pines, followed by three more performances. Miss Anderson in a blood red robe gave a memorable imterpretation of the tragic heroine and was so impressed by the work that she set out to convince her New York producers to present it there with an all professional cast.

In that she was not successful but in 1945 her persistence convinced a New York producer, Jed Harris, that she should do a Greek drama. However his choice was the role of *Media*, one of the bloodiest roles he could have chosen. She agreed to take on such a role but was not satisfied with any of the versions of *Media* in English.

On the basis of her experience in Carmel acting in Jeffers' "The Tower beyond Tragedy" she was convinced that the only person to make a modern translastion of Euripedes' tragedy for the modern theatre was Robin Jeffers. When she had brought Jed Harris around to her way of thinking she still had to persuade Jeffers to undertake the task. Because he had long had an interest in the Greek *Media* and had been impressed with Judith Anderson's performance in "The Tower..." he agreed to undertake the task.

The book of the play *Media* in Jefferson's English version appeared in 1946 and the play opened on October 20, 1947 in the National Theatre in New York with Judith Anderson in the title role. The reception of the play in the tryouts in Princeton and Philadelphia had been so successful that Judith was able to get Robin and Una to come to New York for the opening. As the star took 13 curtain calls the cry of "Author, author" continued to come from the audience. Judith looked up to the box where Robin and Una sat, motioning for him to come to the stage. He remained seated where he was for a time but then stood up by his seat to share the applause.

Judith Anderson with Robin Jeffers at the Carmel Forest Theatre in 1941. (Courtesy of the Carmel Pine Cone and the Judith Anderson Collection)

The play continued to attract full houses for many months and was reviewed in nearly every newspaper and magazine in the country, with a two-page spread in *Life* magazine. Miss Anderson insisted that Jeffers share in the publicity as playwright and receive his generous royalty whenever she appeared in the play.

On road tour *Media* was performed across the United States and Decca Records brought out a "Media Album" of the drama. After its production at the Edinburgh Festival in 1948 it played throughout Britain and was translated into four languages for productions in Denmark, Germany, France and Italy. Jeffers rejoiced that the appreciation of poetry by the average person was furthered through this poetic drama that was being enjoyed by thousands.

Through the success of *Media* a modicum of fortune came to Jeffers and much wider fame. Donnan Jeffers, one of his twin sons, recalls the visitors that came to Tor House to meet the poet. In addition to the many sightseers who came by in buses to have the home of the famous poet pointed out, "Famous people from all walks of life seldom came to Carmel without paying a visit to Tor House."

In his book on the building of Tor House Donnan Jeffers listed poets and writers, Edna St. Vincent Millay, Edgar Lee Masters and Arthur Davidson Ficks as visitors he recalled. Among the Motion Picture actors that he remembered were Charles Chaplin, James Cagney, and Roland Young and of actors on the legitimate stage, Mrs. Patrick Campbell and, of course, Judith Anderson. He had met there also the great humanitarian of Hull House, Jane Addams, the noted humorist, Irvin S. Cobb, the dancer Martha Graham, the flyer Charles Lindberg and his wife, and figures of the musical world as diverse as Leopold Stokowski and George Gershwin.

In February of the year after the opening of *Media* in New York Una was taken to the Stanford

University Hospital for a recurrence of the cancer which had been considered to be cured in 1941. She was released from the hospital in late march but was never without pain until her death in september 1950. In a long poem *Hungerfield*, written soon after Una's death, one short verse was reminiscent of the love poems for Una that were in Jeffers' first published work:

> It is not that I am lonely for you. I am lonely;
> I am mutilated, for you were part of me;
> But men endure that. I am growing old and my love is gone;
> That's not the cry. My torment is memory
> My grief to have seen the banner and beauty of your brave life
> Dragged in the dust down the dim road to death.
> To have seen you defeated,
> You who never despaired, through weakness and pain---to nothing.

In his sorrowing last years the fame of Robinson Jeffers and of his work was spreading. The Librairie Theatrale in Paris published the French translation of *Media* and a German adaptation was made by Eva Hesse which was played throughout Germany and Switzerland with the published version having a wide sale in those countries. In Czechoslovakia Kamil Bodnar translated one of Jeffers' poems as *The Loving Shepherdess* of which a 5,000 copy edition was said to have been sold out in two days. Back in the United States Random House brought out a reprint of *Media* which sold over 8,000 copies.

In 1958 the Voice of America presented *Tower Beyond Tragedy* in Vienna while Judith Anderson was making a sixteen week tour of Australia in *Media.* And *Media* was presented by David Susskind as the offering of the televieion series, "Play of the Week" with Miss Anderson in the leading role, of course. The title of Dame Commander of the British Empire was bestowed

The family group of the Jeffers with Dame Judith Anderson from left to right: Donnan Jeffers and his wife Lee, Robinson, Dame Judith and Una. (Courtesy of the donnan and Garth Jeffers Collection)

on Dame Judith in 1960 by her majesty, Queen Elizabeth II.

But the poet, back in Carmel, was gradually losing his sight until in 1961, when he could no longer decipher his own handwriting, he was wont to speak of himself as "the half-blinded hawk". On January 20, 1962, ten days before his 75th birthday, he died in the bed by the sea-window in the downstairs bedroom of Tor House.

The story of Carmel's towering poet was not ended in 1962, for six years later there was formed "The Robinson Jeffers Tor House Foundation, Inc." The first aim of those who established the Foundation was, as one commentator put it, "to save one of the primary symbols of California culture -- the single most significant literary monument in the state."

The Foundation was able to buy the Tor House and Hawk Tower property and to raise an endowment for its preservation and care as "a catalyst for poets, scholars and poets" so that "its magic can and will become the focal point for the enrichment of poetry in America." The Tor House is open for limited viewing each Friday and Saturday from 10:00 A.M. to 4:00 P.M.

Bibliographical Notes

This chapter has been based on information to be found in the definitive biography, *The Stone Mason of Tor House, The life and Work of Robinson Jeffers* by Melba Berry Bennett (The Ward Ritchie Press, 1966). Melba Bennett was chosen by Una to be Jeffers' biographer. She had access to all the family papers before the death of Una and after that served as an assistant to Robinson in organizing all the available material on his life and work. Other early sources of special value include *Robinson Jeffers, The Man and the Artist* by George Sterling (1926 Boni & Liveright, N. Y.). *Of Una Jeffers* by Edith Greenan (1939, The Ward Ritchie Press), *Una and Robin* by Mabel Dodge Luhan (1976 Friends of the Bancroft Library Univ. of California) based on notes made by the author in 1933. Two interesting small booklets written by Donnan Jeffers, *Some Notes on the Building of Tor House* and *The Stones of Tor House* are available through the Tor House Foundation. Page Stegner is now working on a comprehensive critical biography of Robinson Jeffers under a grant from the Gugenheim Foundation.

IX. Carmel's Theatre of the Golden Bough

Carmel gained national prominence in the Little Theatre movement in the 20s through its Theatre of the Golden Bough built in 1924 by Edward Kuster, a new arrival in town. A description of the theatre complex in Carmel-by-the-Sea was written by Daisy Bostick for the magazine section of *San Francisco Bulletin* and reprinted in *The Pine Cone* on April 24th of that year.

She wrote, in part, "In Carmel-by-the-Sea there is a group of little shops that might well be transferred to an artist's canvas and labeled ' A bit of Old Europe'. They have curving, graceful roofs, some with mottled colors, some are thatched (or made to appear so, Ed.), some reflecting copper tints when the sun filters through the pine trees. There are hooded doorways, unexpected glimpses of little turrets, projecting nooks in walls and floors at irregular heights."

Of the effect that this complex of buildings was to have on the subsequent appearance of the business district of Carmel, Perry Newberry, editor of *The Pine Cone,* wrote a few years later, "We nominate Edward Gerhard Kuster to Carmel's Hall of Fame,not only because of his Theatre of the Golden Bough and the plays presented there, but because he's the one man responsible for the building of unique and different shops in Carmel".

"When Kuster began, in 1923, to design the plans for his Little Theatre he also designed at the same time a group of artistic shops at the corner of Ocean Avenue and Monte Verde Street. They met with public approval apparently for it was not long after this until there were other little shops built in this style. So, instead of the white front wooden buildings that are characteristic of every small town in the west, Kuster's dream - made into reality - has changed our main street into an Ocean Avenue of beauty and artistry."

Today, the quaint look of Carmel's whole business district is due to the continuing influence of the architectural vision of Kuster. Those buildings which have had such a favorable influence on the way that Carmel's shops have been built since that day are still to be seen on the southwest corner of Ocean and Monte Verde, from the half-timbered corner building to the small Candy Cottage which stands at the front of what is now known as 'The Court of the Golden Bough'.

The Theatre of the Golden Bough complex on Ocean Ave. at Monte Verde St. as it appeared in 1924. (Courtesy of Mrs. Marcia Kuster Rider)

The original golden bough symbol which marked the place of the theatre was described by Bostick, "Over the sidewalk marking the entrance to the stone pathway between two of these shops, and projecting from a tree, is an old wrought iron sign representing a graceful bough, its leaves following the double curve of the line of beauty."

The name chosen for the theatre as represented by this symbol was explained by Bostick in this way:

"The legend of the Golden Bough was so widespread among the ancients of every clime that it may well be regarded as one of the basic myths of the human race. It has to do with the wandering of Aeneas after the fall of Troy. When bidden by the Sibyl to seek his father, Anchises, in the Elysian fields, he was advised that the only possibe passport to those dim regions was a golden bough from a certain sacred grove, most difficult to approach.

"Many of our classic myths are built around this thought and through them runs a common thread -- that the golden spray or branch was a key to the world of imagination and fantasy. Hence the aptness of the name for an institution which from its inception will join in the growth of imaginative theatre in this country."

The wrought iron representation of a bough which marked the entrance to the Theatre of the Golden Bough is now a prized possession of Mrs. Marcia Kuster Rider, daughter of the late Edward Kuster. (Photograph by Marguerite Temple)

Unfortunately nothing remains today of the theatre itself which was in the area now included in the Golden Bough Court and extending out into the parking area of the Spinning Wheel Motel. Some idea of the style of the theatre, which was built "to follow the line of the semi-pagan architecture", which Kuster had admired in Italy, may be seen in the part of the forecourt which remains. The beautiful plaster frieze can be seen across the front of the former lobby area, continuing around the corner over the original steps and along the outer wall of the former theatre.

The quaint building which housed a weaving shop and is now a sweet shop still stands in the forecourt. In the back corner of this there remains the original theatre box office, now partly hidden by a thin growth of shrubs. Two other shops now occupy the remaining part of the original building. The foyer of the theatre was entered through the archway between the shops.

There was space in the theatre for 800 persons in usual theatre seating but here the audience was limited to half that number because specially built upholstered rattan armchairs were set in well spaced rows, making this the most comfortable theatre in America.

Upon entering the theatre one would be struck with the beauty of the room with its cove ceiling rising forty feet above the floor. The forestage which projected twenty feet out from the great proscenium arch, was an adaptation of the *Orkhestra*, the dancing space of the ancient Greek amphitheatre. There was no exposed orchestra pit, but instead a music room was located under the forestage with sound entering the theatre through concealed ports in the risers of the full width steps. A masked periscope showed the entire stage action on a scren in the music room below.

Of the completed theatre Irving Pichel was to write in the *San Francisco Daily News,* "There can be no

The original boxoffice of the First Golden Bough Theatre as it appears today, with Sydney Temple at the window. (Photograph by Margurite Temple)

question that the Theatre of the Golden Bough is the loveliest theatre in America. It has been declared the most beautiful small theatre, but I know of none larger to compare with it in beauty." And Maurice Brown, with his knowledge of theatres in Europe, went even further. In the November, 1924 issue of the periodical, *Drama*, he called the new Golden Bough "the loveliest and best equipped theatre of its size in America -- or, so far as I know, with the exception of

A view of the interior of the first Golden Bough Theatre. (Courtesy of the Hathaway Collection)

the Cologne Exposition Theatre, in the world."

Edward Kuster, creator of the Theatre of the Golden Bough and its school of drama, had been an attorney in Los Angeles who had long had an interest in the theatre, acting small parts in the Majestic Theatre there. When his firm had won so large a case against the three transcontinental railroads coming into Los Angeles that he was able to retire at an early age, he moved to Carmel. He came in 1920 because he found that here was "a little village that was simply boiling over with theatre-mindedness."

Soon after the theatre was completed a Summer School of Dramatic Art was instituted at the theatre with Maurice Browne as Director. A product of an English 'public school' and Cambridge University,

Browne had migrated to Chicago where he had built up a theatrical tradition in the Chicago Little Theatre which was the precursor of the Little Theatre movement all over the United States. Known throughout the land as 'the father of the Little Theatre' Brown was now conducting a school of drama in San Francisco. Kuster attended the sessions of that school and found that this was just the sort of training that he desired for the Little Theatre that he was developing in Carmel.

Browne was persuaded to move to Carmel and to bring with him as the faculty for the School of Theatre there his wife, Ellen Von Volkengerg, the actress, Hedwiga Reicher, one of Max Reinhardt's leading ladies, and Rose Bogdanoff, a New York scenic designer. For several years summer classes in the arts had been offered by the Arts and Crafts Club but this was the first time that so prominent a faculty had been gathered in Carmel.

The students and faculty of the first session of the Golden Bough School of Drama gathered on the steps which still exist beside the former foyer of the theatre. Kuster is at the far left between two of the faculty members; Browne is above to the left of another. (Courtesy of Ms. Lucille Kiester of the staff of the old theatre)

One of the scholarship students, Jadwiga Noskowiak, who lived with the Kusters while attending the theatre school, now lives in The Hacienda in the Carmel Valley. Her daughter, Barbara Babcock, has followed in her mother's footsteps and won the Emmy Award for 1981 as the best actress in a TV series for her part in "Hill Street Blues".

Mrs. Babcock tells of one unforgettable experience that she had at the Golden Bough when she was taking the part of Little Eva in the production of "Uncle Tom's Cabin." For her ascent into heaven she was wired to a hoist connected to the sky-dome over the stage. Unfortunately for her the young man who operated the hoist was attempting to have a romance with the youthful star and whenever she didn't respond to his advances he would take out his frustrations by giving her a severe jerk as he pulled her into 'heaven'.

Jadwiga Noskowiak as Little Eva being lifted into heaven in the Golden Bough production of *Uncle Tom's Cabin.* (Courtesy of Mrs. Jadwiga Noskowiak Babcock)

In addition to providing entertainment for the community the plays presented at the Golden Bough were to provide another sort of 'drama' as more thought-provoking plays were offered. In January of 1926 the Berkeley Playhouse Players came to the theatre with Eugene O'Neill's *All God's Chillun Got Wings.* The play, built around the problem presented by a black man marrying a white woman, was too *avant garde* for the time and led to some distress among the Carmelites. As one reviewer commented, after reviewing the plot and the divisions that it caused among those who had attended the performance, "And so, there is the play. Like it or not, you cannot be quite the same after you have seen it. Only a big play can have that effect."

At another time Kuster's presentation of O'Neill's *The Hairy Ape* raised the threat of theatre censorship in Carmel. The drama was called "a swearing nightmare true to its name" in one letter to *The Pine Cone.* Another play, *They Knew What They Wanted,* was so criticised for the swearing in it that at a meeting of the members of the Community Church a resolution was passed to the effect that "any production offensive to a considerable and representative group of the town should not be considered a community enterpise." Since the latter play had been presented on February 11th, a comic valentine poem appeared in *The Pine Cone* address "To Edward Kuster"

The rose is red
The violet blue,
The community Church
Is after you.
You've made them all
Sit up and gape
They Knew What They Wanted
The Hairy Ape.

Twenty five plays were presented at the Golden Bough Theatre in 1924, the year of Carmel's Little Theatre 'explosion' in addition to the plays at the Arts and Crafts Theatre and the summer program at the Forest Theatre. But Carmel was coming near the saturation point in theatricals as the influence of the Depression came to be felt.

It was in December of 1925 that the Arts and Crafts Club leased their theatre to George Ball, a young Golden Bough player who had come to Carmel with Maurice Browne. Ball changed the name of his theatre to The Carmel Playhouse and sought to upgrade the calibre of the performances there to compete with the Golden Bough. Next Kuster had announced in April of that year that "carefully selected" motion pictures would be shown on Friday and Saturday nights in addition to the regular program of live drama in an attempt to make the theatre pay.

Two years later he took off for Europe with his new wife, Gabrielle, in order to study production techniques in Berlin which was then known as the fountainhead of contemporary and classical theatre. Having spoken German since his childhood in a German colony in Indiana, he was also seeking new plays to translate for his Carmel theatre. He rented the Golden Bough to an artistic pair, Dene Denney and Hazel Watross, who were to use the theatre for musical concerts as well as drama. These two were to establish the Carmel Music Society and to institute the Carmel Bach Festival which remains a part of Carmel's cultural life.

When Kuster returned from Europe in 1929, as he was later to recall, "with my pockets full of plays and my head of ideas", he found that the Arts and Crafts Theatre on Monte Verde, having gone through difficult days, was for sale at an attractive price. The Abalone Baseball League had tried to make a go of it as a money raiser and had failed. So he bought it. Now he had two theatres with the Depression deepening and motion picture houses crowding out legitimate theatres all over the land.

The solution to his problem came when he was approaced by a movie chain with a generous offer for a five year lease on his Ocean Avenue Theatre. He leased that original Golden Bough Theatre to David Bolton of the Golden State Theatre in Monterey with the stipulation that the name "Golden Bough" could not be used for the movie house. That then became known as the "Carmel Theatre" and Kuster moved his activities to his newly acquired theatre on Monte Verde which he renamed "The Studio Theatre of the Golden Bough" and remodelled with a new stage, a new seating and new lighting.

Remembering that move, Kuster said, "it was the beginning of 1930. Then began what I honestly believe to have been the golden period of Carmel play production. I had full community support for my new venture." The first of the dramas that he presented there was one that he was translating from the German. When rehearsals started he was still completing the translation of what he called *The Thrip'ny Opera*, characterized by him as "a strange concoction of satire, sardonic humor and haunting Kurt Weil music."

Presented at the Golden Baugh Studio Theatre the play was to continue for seven nights, the maximum period for which Kuster had obtained play rights, to enthusiastic audiences. It was nearly thirty years later that the translation, billed with a slightly different title, *The Threepenny Opera,* was to become a great success in New York. *Karl and Anna* and *the Beggar on Horseback* were among the other German dramas that Kuster brought back from Berlin to have American premiers in Carmel.

By 1935 he was anxious to revive the original Golden Bough Theatre on Ocean as a part time Little Theatre, plays being produced periodically there along with the continuing program of motion pictures. So, when the five year lease ran out, he refused a renewal of the lease unless an arrangement was made whereby the Golden Bough Players could perform a stage play in his beloved original theatre once a month.

Setting to work with a will Kuster and his Carmel Players put the stage, dressing rooms, orchestra room and stage lighting facilities back into first class condition for the revival. *By Candlelight,* a play which he had translated from the German, was chosen as the first production of the new series.

The cast was assembled, rehearsals completed and on Friday night, May 17, 1935, *By Candlelight* described as "a sprightly continental comedy of errors", was presented to an overflow crowd at 11:00 PM after the movie. It appeared that Little Theatre in Carmel was to be reborn where it had been promoted with such promise eleven years before.

What happened next was described by Ted Kuster in an address that he made to the Carmel Woman's Club in 1960. "On the next day the lessees had their matinee and evening showing as usual. Then on Sunday evening, May 19th, at 6:30, a green car was seen by a gardener across the street to stop near the stage entrance on Monte Verde Street. He dragged his hose around to the rear garden so was away from the street for a time. When he returned after about 20 minutes the green car was gone, one of the double doors of the stage entrance was open and smoke and flames were pouring out... The theatre was completely destroyed except for the lobby which stands and has been converted into some small shops. Deficient water supply and insufficient water pressure made the ruin of the structure a certainty...subsequently the city installed larger water mains on Ocean Avenue."

One of America's most beautiful theatres had been destroyed, never to be rebuilt on Carmel's main street. As Kuster was later to relate, "The Depression was still with us, rent for the Golden Bough was at an end and I had to get busy. I had little insurance - for

Carmel's fire truck parked by the small water hydrant on Ocean Avenue as the Golden Bough Theatre burned down. (Courtesy of the Hathaway Collection)

we had cut down on insurance so as to be able to get a maximum of income from the properties. Luckily the surrounding shops suffered no damage... I used the small insurance money in fitting out the little Monte Verde Street Playhouse with the best motion picture equipment on the market." Renamed The Filmarte Theatre he leased the building for five years for the showing of 'art films'.

But again in 1940 Kuster took over the management of that theatre, renaming it The Golden Bough Playhouse. For the next nine years he operated this as a combination house, producing stage plays on

Monday nights and continuing to show 'quality motion pictures' the other nights of the week. Each stage play ran for six consecutive Mondays - an arrangement that the amatuer actors liked and that made for a full house each Monday night.

This arrangement of plays alternating with motion pictures continued at the second 'Golden Bough', the Playhouse of the Golden Bough, until well into 1949. Then as told in Kuster's words, "All went merrily until April, 1949, when some being from the lower regions prompted Lloyd Weer to suggest that we repeat *By Candlelight.* Lloyd was Carmel's best actor for years. He had been leading man for *By Candlelight* when the original Golden Bough burned down in 1935. His idea was that we were all getting older and pretty soon wouldn't fit the roles we had played before. Well, we got the gang together - there were only seven in the cast - and started rehearsals."

As he was ruefully to recall, "Dozens of people told us, sometimes jocularly, sometimes seriously, that we were tempting fate, Providence and what have you to dare to put on the play again, but we laughed off all the gloomy warnings... My son, Colin, then 18, reminded me of the joy of the firebug in seeing the engines come down the street and the crowd gather, etcetera. He asked me to hire a special watchman for the theatre for a couple of weeks. Well, I put my son in his place all right on that.

"We went right on and we performed the play before a delighted audience on Monday night, May 17th, '49...In the early hours of the following Friday morning I heard, as in a dream, heavy knocking on the door and the barking of our dogs. And in a few moments my wife roused me to announce that once more a Golden Bough theatre had been destroyed."

So twice a Carmel theatre owned by Kuster had been burned down within a few days of the opening of the drama *By Candlelight.* Twenty-five years after the first Golden Bough Theatre had opened Carmel was without a Little Theatre. Arson was suspectd as the cause of the second fire at a Kuster Golden Bough, as it had been in the first, fourteen years before. In this case the lock on one of the doors of the Playhouse was found to have been pried open - evidence that forcible entry had been made by someone determined to burn down the Playhouse.

In order to protect the town's Sunset Auditorium from a similar fate the City Council of Carmel decreed that there should be no more live candlelight on Carmel stages. That decree was to "prohibit open flame on any stage or in the rooms or corridors adjacent thereto...and no-smoking rules in force on or around any stage or dressing rooms adjacent thereto." So something good did come in the enactment of this which came to be called Carmel's "Candlelight Decree."

By the beginning of 1950 Kuster came up with a plan by which a third Golden Bough Theatre would arise like a Phoenix from its fiery destructions. For this a stock company was formed with the Kuster family taking common stock and preferrd stock to be sold to raise money for the building. The stock sold well and Kuster announced a program of summer plays for 1950 in the Sunset Auditorium, the proceeds to go for lighting and scenic equipment in the yet-to-be-built theatre.

A new problem arose as the owners of property on Monte Verde petitioned the Planning Commission to rezone the location of the former Playhouse to private residence. Among other arguments residents argued that the parking problem for a theatre in that location would be considerable. That the position was well taken can be seen today as Monte Verde is filled with parked cars in that area for the seven and nine o'clock shows.

The Planning Commision decided that the property owners had no recourse for the theatre zoning had been long established. A conciliatory meeting was held by Kuster with the residents and an agreement was reached by which the new theatre would be of about the size and appearance of the former playhouse.

By the time that the building was completed more than 300 families owned stock in the theatre, most of them residents of Carmel. The stockholders were invited to be the first night audience on October 2, 1952 when the third Golden Bough Theatre opened with the Monterey Symphony Orchestra performing on the deep stage.

The Kuster family at the opening of the third Golden Bough Theatre with Edward G. Kuster and his wife Gabrielle seated with their children Colin and Marcia above. (Photograph of Arthur McEwen)

Ever interested in new technique of the theatre Kuster had a theatre-in-the-round to seat 150 persons below the deep stage of the main auditorium. This small theatre which has its entrance on Casanova Street was to have a large part in the future of Little Theatre in Carmel. Though Kuster had not been able to build two new theatres as he had hoped, one for motion pictures on Ocean Avenue and the other for legitimate theatre on Monte Verde Street, he did end up with a large theatre on Monte Verde which was to be mainly a picture house and an intimate theatre with its entrance on Casanova for Little Theatre productions.

The Circle Theatre on Casanova Street as it appears today. (Photograph by Marguerite Temple)

Called The Circle Theatre, the theatre on Casanova Street continued as an active legitimate theatre for many years. For a part of the time Kuster's son-in-law, Fred Rider, served as the Theatre manager there. When in 1967 the Carmel Building Inspector ruled that the electric wiring was unsafe and must be replaced but the cost of such was beyond the means of those in charge. Since that time there have been no public performances in the Circle Theatre.

This success of the Circle Theatre before 1967 made it possible to let the Monte Verde theatre to be used exclusively for motion pictures. It was leased to the United California Theatres, a motion picture theatre chain, until 1965 when the whole building was sold to that compnay and the Circle Theatre rented back to the Circle players-until the theatre in-the-round was forced to close two years later.

The Golden Bough Cinema as it stands today on Monte Verde Street. (Photograph by Marguerite Temple)

Edward Gerhard Kuster, builder of Carmel's three Golden Bough theatres died of a heart attack at the age of 83 on September 7, 1961, in Lugano, Switzerland while on a holiday with his wife.

Bibliographical Notes

The Historical Collection at the Harrison Memorial Library of Carmel has much valuable material on the Golden Bough Years including several articles printed on Edward Kuster during his life and a very full accout of *The Carmel Theatre from 1910 to 1935* by Morgan Evans Stock (1952). This is a poor copy of the typed thesis that Stock presented to the Department of Speech and Drama of Stanford University in connection with a degree of Master of Arts. It was based on contemporary records and personal interviews with Edward Kuster, Herbert Heron and others who had been active in Carmel's Little Theatre movement.

Other works which throw light on this period in Carmel include the very valuable *Carmel at Work and Play* by Daisy F. Bostick and Dorothea Castelhun, first published in 1925 and reissued in 1977 by Lacy Williams Faia and *Too Late to Lament,* the story of his life in Little Theatre by Maurice Browne (1956) plus the filmstrips of *The Carmel Pine Cone.*

X. Carmel's Attractions Bring Growth

The reputation of Carmel-by-the-Sea as a unique community of California and of the nation was growing in the years after the First World War. But the village continued its battle to remain unchanged as it fought 'progress'. It was said that "All in all Carmel has used more energy to remain unpretentious than most small towns use in striving to become business centers". And the battle continues to the time of the writing of this book.

An editorial in *The Pine Cone* for May 11, 1922, entitled "Status Quo Ante" expressed the attitude which existed from that day to this. In comparing Greenwich Village in New York with Carmel-by-the-Sea in california as two centers of art on opposite sides of the continent the editorial drew attention to the difference in development between the two, "While Greenwich Village was finding itself invaded by the vandals of business and manufacturing, in Carmel-by-the-Sea the artistic element was winning by keeping Carmel 'different'."

It was stated that "Because they are narrow and tree-dotted and winding, side-walk less and bumpy, Carmel's street are still different. Its beach without a hurdy-gurdy to vie with the music of the surf is different." And the residents were determined to keep it that way.

Even the suggestion that houses in town be numbered so that mail could be delivered was met with another editorial titled "What Next, a Subway?" In which it was urged that such 'cityfying' be turned down because "going for the mail is an institution in Carmel." And, though mail is delivered in R. F. D. boxes to houses outside one square mile of the city limits, those living within the city boundaries still go to the Post Office to get their mail and to meet their neighbors there.

Yet Carmel's attractiveness, its defence of its

uniqueness, continued to attract more residents who were seeking this sort of place. This influx brought the need for more housing and in the post-war boom several areas were developed for housing outside the original boundaries of the incorporated town.

In 1922 the "Carmel Woods", a 125 acre subdivision on the north side of town was put on the market. Next came the sale of 233 acres of homesites in "'Hatton Fields', developed on the road of the former Hatton Estate.

Then, in the following year Mr. and Mrs. Willis Walker purchased 216 acres of the Martin Ranch to the south, extending to the region of the Carmel River. Developed as the Walker Tract, this is now known as 'The Point', the area over-looking the bird preserve in the water flats of the river.

That the area was beginning to attract some of the most famous of the Motion Picture stars was evident when it was announced that Douglas Fairbank and his new bride, Mary Pickford, had bought a 1,000 acre tract for a hunting lodge in the Jolon Valley in the Santa Lucia Mountains to the south of Carmel.

Then, on November 25, 1920, there appeared the headline, "Movies Start Grinding on Point Lobos Sunday." In that article it was stated that "Eric Von Stroheim has paid Carmel a hundred thousand dollar compliment in the selection of Point Lobos for the film 'Foolish Wives' in which Pauline Frederick stars."

In a front page box the excitement caused by the filming was commented on: "Many of San Francisco's social set motored from the Del Monte Hotel last Sunday, arriving early among the pines and cypresses of Point Lobos, and mingled with the paid Dukes and Duchesses awaiting their arrival on the terraces of the casino, overlooking the blue waters of Carmel Bay."

Whether the picture was to have a great success at the Box Office, or not, it had already been approved by the Carmelites who were ready to admit, with their

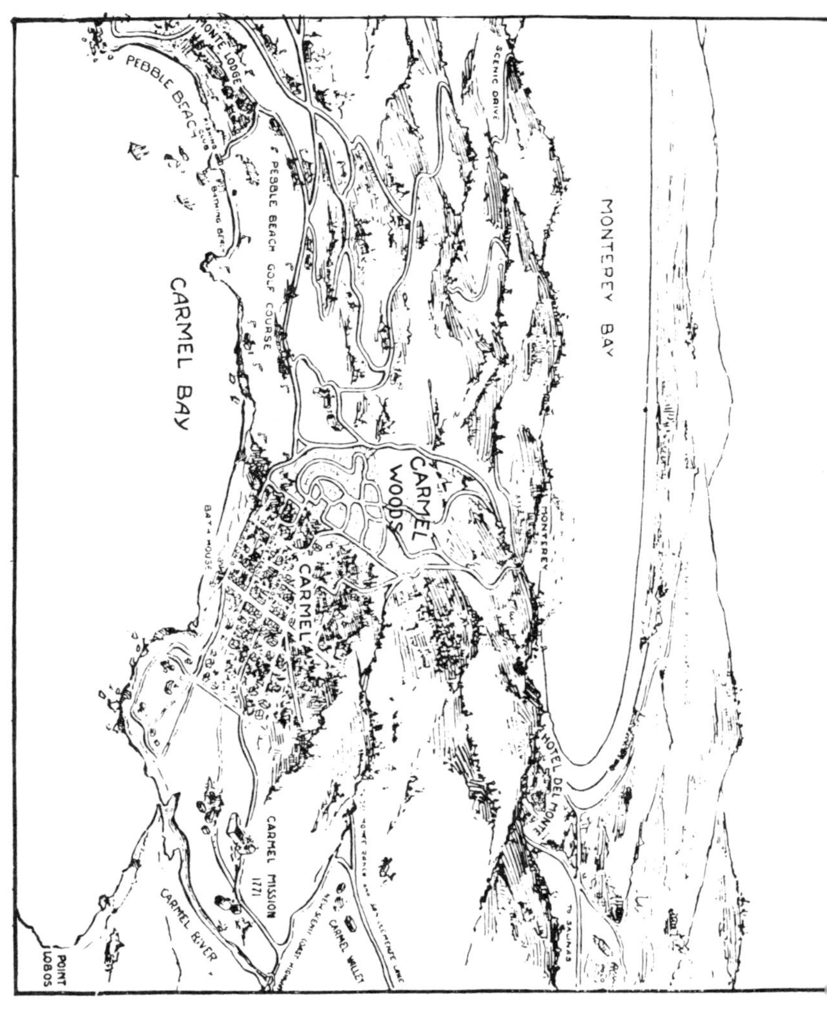

A drawing of Carmel and the Monterey Pininsula with Monterey Bay beyond showing the new development of Carmel Woods. (Courtesy of the Harrison Memorial Library of Carmel)

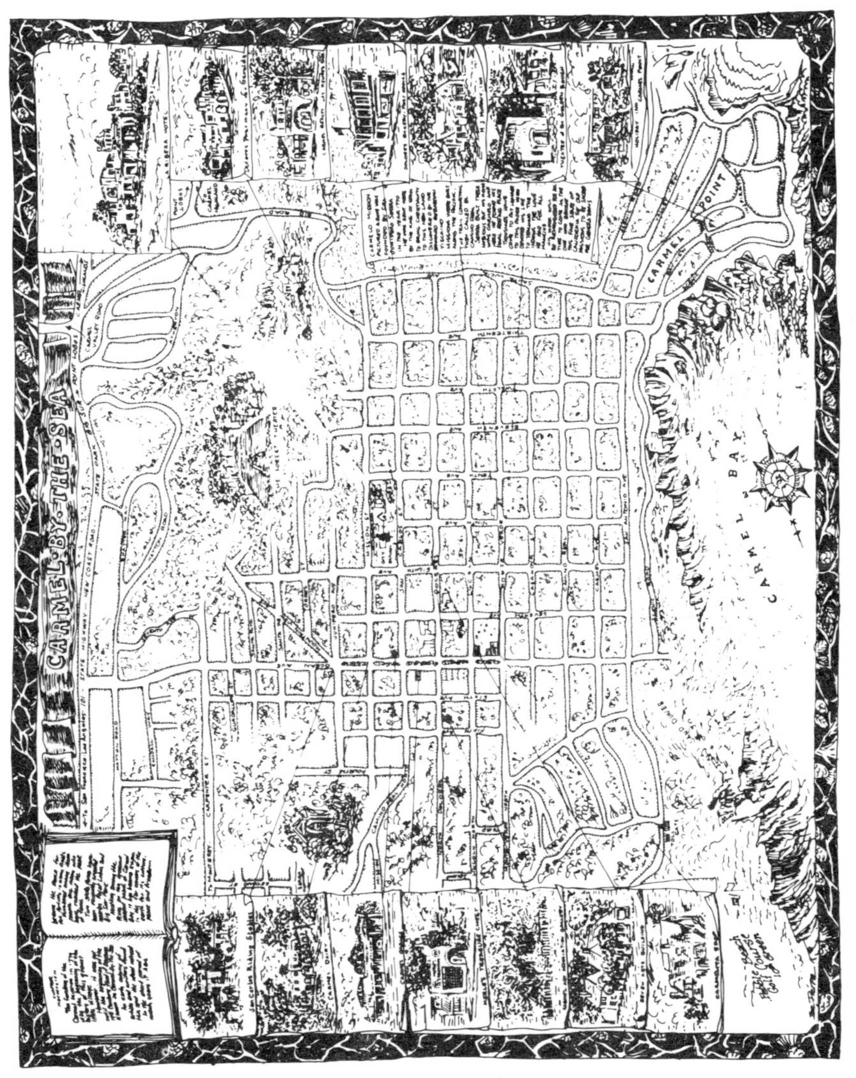

A sketch of Carmel showing Carmel Woods, Hatton Fields and Carmel Point additions. (Courtesy of the Harrison Memorial Library of Carmel)

usual lack of excessive modesty, "The people of Carmel, who are truly cosmopolitan, and perhaps better qualified to pass judgment on artistic effects than any other community, are favorably impressed with the preliminaries of the production of 'Foolish Wives', but await its completion and presentation to the public to answer the question of its acceptance."

The town has continued to attract notable members of the Motion Picture and entertainment communities. As this book is being written Carmel and its immediate neighborhood include as residents Jean Arthur, Doris Day, Kim Novack, Betty White, Merv Griffin, Paul Anka and Alan Funt. And in 1986 Clint Eastwood, a resident who own a restaurant in town, was elected mayor of Carmel-by-the-Sea in 1986.

The reproduction of the Monte Carlo Casino was built on Point Lobos for the motion picture, "Foolish Wives" for which Eric Von Stroheim was the producer-director, Pauline Frederick the star. (Courtesy of the Monterey County Library)

Through the years the area has also attracted less desirable elements, particularly in the days of Prohibition. It was in 1926 that a rum runner, *The Ocean Queen,* was abandoned in Whalers Cove of Point Lobos and impounded by the Coast Guard. The thirty miles of rugged coastline and open sea south of Carmel were difficult to patrol, so provided an ideal place for the landing of illegal liquor for the San Francisco and Los Angeles markets. Though there were several places along the shore for secret landings, Whaler's Cove was the most protected and a small rum runners boat anchored there would attract little attention among the many small boats of the abalone canning company located in the Cove.

The remains of the rum-runners boat in front of the whale skeleton as they were once set on the shore of Whalers Cove. (Courtesy of Point Lobos State Reserve)

A small boat coming from a rendezvous with a larger ship at sea would be met at the Cove landing dock by limousines that, when filled with bootleg 'booze', would rumble away in the night for distant locations. On June 20, 1922 Federal Agents surprised a group of rum-runners in the Cove. It was said that nearly 100 rounds were traded between the agents and the whiskey traders. Eight men were captured and 15 vehicles taken, from the limousines to moving vans.

One small rum-runner boat that had burned to the water line in the cove was placed on the shore by A. M. Allen, owner of Point Lobos, after the point was opened to tourists. With the rum runners boat was displayed the skeleton of a forty foot whale until tourist depedations and weathering in the winter storms broke it into pieces. Some of the pieces of the whale skeleton can still be seen behind the cabin that is in place on the shore of the cove.

In 1926 Carmel experienced both a forest fire in the hills above Carmel Valley and a rather severe earthquake that shook up the townspeople. In the early hours of Friday, October 22nd, the shaking brought Carmelites out of their homes. It was reported in *The Pine Cone*, "The costumes seen on Ocean Avenue were delightful. Robert Stanton appeared in a pair of blue and orange awning striped pajamas and waited to see if the hotel Mont Verde would collapse. He seemed rather disappointed when it didn't for he had predicted that it would." In the next month some 600 acres of the Los Aurelles Ranch and the Hatton and Sheehy Ranches were burned in an extensive fire.

But a Los Angeles evangelist, Aimee Semple McPherson, was to bring more fame, or noteriety, to Carmel than rum runners, fire and earthquake. Aimee, as she was called by one and all, had arrived in Los Angeles in 1921 at the head of a cross-country tent revival. By 1923 her Angelus Temple, seating 5,000, had been contructed at a cost of a million and a half dollars, realized from contributions to her continued revival crusades.

Carmel came into her story after she vanished while surf bathing at Ocean Park, near Los Angeles, in May 1926. Six weeks later she walked in from the Arizona desert with a tale of having been abducted by two desperados named Jake and Mexican Rose.

According to her story she had broken a window in the shack where she was held when her captors passed out from drinking mescal, the strong cactus liquor. She had then run across the desert, according to her story, for several day before she reached help.

Aimee Semple McPherson as she preached in her Angelus Temple and broadcast over radio station KFSG. (From a publicity Photograph)

Doubt began to be cast on Aimee's story when it was pointed out that her shoes were unscuffed and her skin unburned by the desert sun. Intrepid reporters were soon to unearth the rumor that she had spent a part of the time that she was missing in a 'love nest' in Carmel with Kenneth G. Ormiston, the former operator of the Temple radio station, KFSG. Because of all the trouble caused to the police department in the search for her during the time of her disappearance the Los Angeles District Attorney brought a charge of obstructing justice against Mrs. McPherson and Ormiston.

When the L. A. District Attorney came to Carmel to investigate the rumor of the 'love nest' he found fourteen Carmelites who could positively identify Ormiston as the man who rented a cottage on Scenic near Ocean Avenue as 'George E. McIntire'. And three persons were willing to swear that they recognized 'Mrs. McIntire' as the famous Los Angeles evangelist. When the trial took place those witnesses enjoyed expense paid visits to Los Angeles for several days and gloried in the public interest that their testimony aroused.

Aimee established a 'Fight the Devil Fund' to pay for her legal defence as she rallied her supporters around her. To any who would doubt her story she replied, "What does it matter that her shoes were unscuffed and her skin unburned? Had not Shedrack, Meshak and Abednego gone through the fiery furnace without harm?" Her followers never doubted her story and the case was dismissed for lack of positive proof. For some time, however, merchants on Ocean Avenue and residents who were shopping there were bothered by being asked by the tourists, "Where's Aimee's cottage?"

Perhaps the noteriety that came to Carmel in this episode had something to do with the growth of new publications that were started in the late 1920's to compete with *The Pine Cone.* In 1926 W. K. Bassett who had newspaper experience in Honolulu and San Francisco established the first competing newspaper, *The Carmel Cymbal.* Other papers were to appear in succeeding years.

The Carmelite began publication in 1928 and *The Carmel Sun* in 1933, followed in turn by *The Villager* and *The California Sun,* later to be named *The Californian.* There was even one attempt at a daily paper, *The Village Daily,* in that period. There was also to be *The Town Crier, The Carmel Cottager, The Pacific Weekly* as well as *Controversy,* as Bassett called his last attempt to establish a paper in Carmel.

Though he failed in his several editorial ventures in Carmel, as did the other owners and editors of these local papers, Bassett will long be remembered by older residents for the EXTRA of his *Carmel Cymbal*, the only 'extra' ever issued in Carmel. The origin of that extra edition and its sale was recalled by Robert Stanton, the Carmel architect, before his recent death as his home in the Carmel Valley.

On May 14, 1927 an article appeared in *The Carmel Cymbal* in which it was announced that a bond issue had been proposed for a recreation center with swimming pool, tennis courts and gymnasium to be built on the Carmel beach at the end of Ocean Avenue where the bathhouse had formerly stood. Because an editorial in that issue had given a reserved endorsement to the project, Stanton went to Bassett and convinced him that he should withdraw the paper's endorsement of the project. And since there was to be a meeting of the Village Trustees (as the Councilmen were then called) to consider the matter on the next day the only thing to do was to put out an extra edition of the weekly paper.

Bassett and Stanton worked through the night writing copy and getting the paper printed so that at dawn the next day the special issue of the *Cymbal* opposing the bond issue and the beach development was ready. Stanton then went up and down Ocean Avenue crying out, "EXTRA, EXTRA" and calling out the key words of the lead article, "Save the Carmel Beach from Santa Cruzitis".

As a result no bond issue was proposed and the

people of Carmel have Stanton and Bassett to thank for the beach which has been preserved in its natural state to this day, without the development that is to be seen in Santa Cruz and other beach cities of California.

The zoning of the town was settled on March 8, 1929, when two zones only were established in the village--zone 1, residential, and zone 2, essential business. The whole beach area was zoned then for private homes.

There are no zones 3 or 4 in Carmel, thus the town has kept out manufacturing and all other "obnoxious industries", including mortuaries. And Carmel has never had a jail.

The uniqueness for Carmel-by-the-Sea has been due to the determination of its citizens and of the Mayor and Councilmen that have been elected. One who was most instrumental in keeping Carmel to be unique was Perry Newberry, a war correspondent in the First World War when he was in France with the Red Cross and later editor of *The Carmel Pine Cone.* Those who live in Carmel and even those who come to the town for short stays to enjoy its uniqueness owe a debt of gratitude to Perry Newberry.

Perry Newberry at the Carmel Bullentin Board on Ocean Avenue (Courtesy of the Monterey County Library)

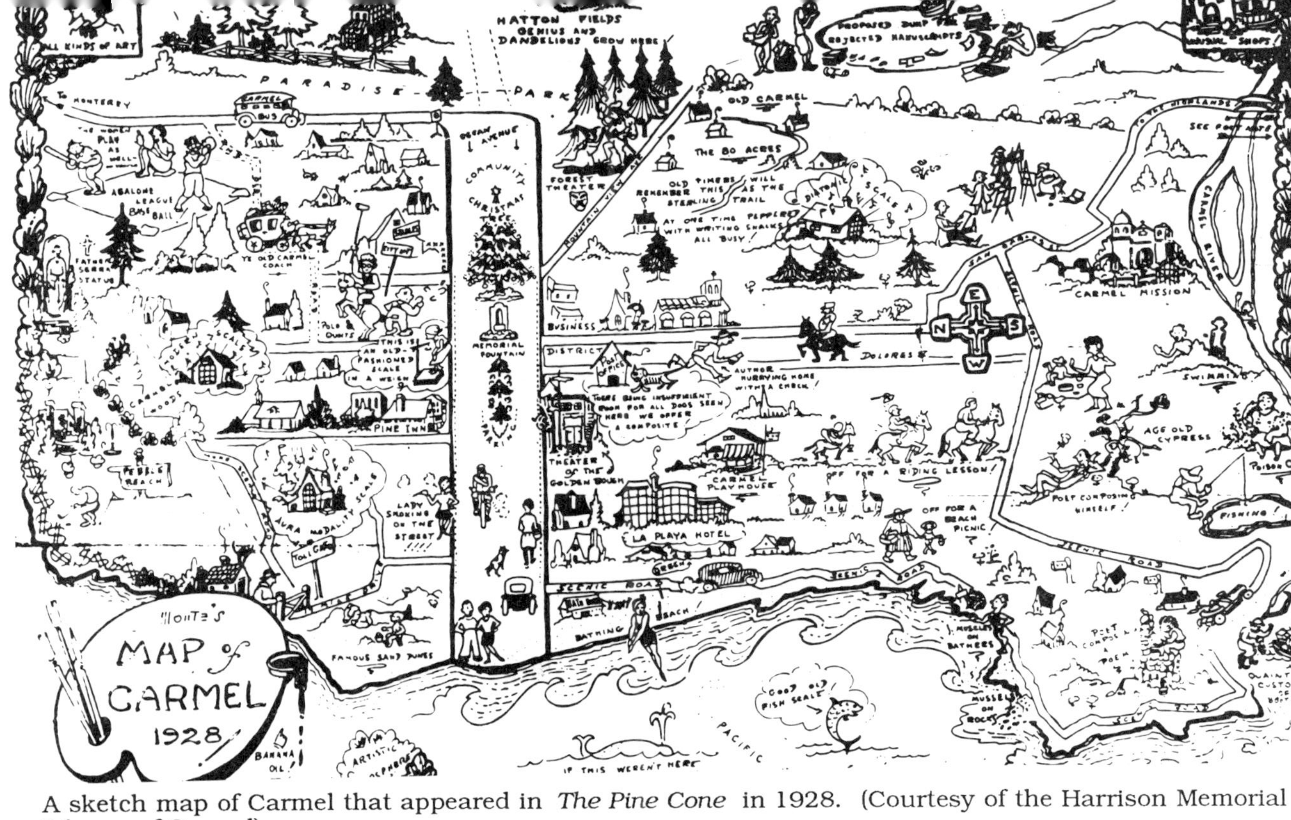

A sketch map of Carmel that appeared in *The Pine Cone* in 1928. (Courtesy of the Harrison Memorial Library of Carmel)

In 1926 Newberry ran for Mayor on a platform that has become a part of Carmel folklore. His placard, attached to the bulletin board on Ocean Avenue read, "Believing that what 9,999 towns out of 10,000 want is just what Carmel doesn't want, I am a candidate on the platform DON'T BOOST! I am making a spirited campaign to win by asking those who disagree with me to vote against me:

> Don't Vote for Perry Newberry
> If you hope to see Carmel become a city.
> If you want its growth boosted.
> If you desire its commercial success.
> If street lamps on its corners mean happiness to you.
> If concrete street pavements represent your civic ambitions.
> If you have less regard for the unique character of Carmel than for the opportunity of money making.
> If you think that a glass factory is of greater value than a sand dune, or a millionaire than an artist, or a mansion than a little brown cottage.
> If you truly want Carmel to become a boosting, hustling, wide-awake lively metropolis,
> DON'T VOTE FOR PERRY NEWBERRY

It was in the depth of the Depression, in February 1933, that the 'Carmel Dollars' were placed in circulation. One thousand of the dollars were printed by the Carmel Business Association to be used to pay for work done by the unemployed of the city on public works. The merchants agreed to accept the Carmel Dollars at face value for merchandise and services.

The 'dollars' were not to be legal tender and were not bankable, of course, but were to circulate freely among Carmelites. A 3-cent Unemployment Relief Stamp was to be affixed to the back and cancelled at each transfer as used. When 36 such stamps had been affixed to the spaces provided on the back, the certificate would be redeemed for one dollar in cash, the additional eight cents covering the cost of printing and issueing. In this way the merchants of

Carmel played their part in helping to relieve the unemployment situation that was being felt in every town in the nation.

The Carmel Dollar designed by Jo Mora and issued by the Carmel Business Association for relief work in Carmel. (Courtesy of the Harrison Memorial Library of Carmel)

It was at this time that Samuel F. B. Morse, who had been involved in the development of the Pebble Beach homesite development, proposed that California's state capital be moved back to its original location - Monterey. In an address at the Sunset Auditorium Morse claimed that Sacramento, which had been made the capital in gold rush days, was no longer at the cneter of the state's interests. Less than half of the state's population was then in a 300 mile radius of Sacremento, he argued, while 90 percent of the of the population was then within a 300 mile radius of Monterey.

This idea struck terror to the hearts of Carmelites and others on the Monterey peninsula. If it would be bad for this quiet area to be like Santa Cruz, it was unthinkable that the metropolization of a state capital should descend on the peninsula. When Morse announced that he had put off the pushing of this idea for a time, an editorial in *The Pine Cone* read, in part,

"We thank you, Sam Morse, for a reprieve in the capital punishment of Carmel by a postponment of execution."

And in an editorial titled "The Lettuce Strike" it was stated "This is the sort of thing that hastens 'The Revolution', but place the blame where it belongs - at the door of the shipper-owners who incite violence and their henchmen, the peace officers." This was perhaps the 'straw in the wind' which would explain the upsetting of local political history when Franklin D. Roosevelt, the Democratic candidate for President of the United States, carried the traditionally Republican town of Carmel by 85 votes.

After a disastrous flood in 1937 it was reported that "most of our dirt roads are in the bay now." At the City Council meeting at that time there was talk of storm sewers but no action. So strong was the feeling among the citizens at this inaction that recall petitions were circulated against the mayor, Everett Smith, and two members of the City Council.

Also upsetting to the residents of Carmel was the possibility that their beloved Forest Theatre would have to be sold off as house lots because of debts that had grown in the Depression years. The property consisted of 16 house lots, each of which was assessed $33 for sewer connections even though no sewers had been connected there, and back property taxes of $2,000 were due in addition to payments on a mortgage.

The Forest Theatre Society got busy with money raising affairs and by January 1937 it was able to offer the property to the city, free of encumbrances, which was the only way that the City Council would accept it, for the stage was rotting and the seats broken. The grounds were then designated a city park, free of taxes, with the understanding that the production of outdoor theatricals should be considered a legitimate park use. But it was of little use without proper stage or seats.

Fortunately in 1938 Herbert Heron, who had

"WHAT PUBLIC?" . . . Mayor Smith

A cartoon which appeared in *The Pine Cone* of August 13, 1937. The members of the Council were: E. S. Everett Smith, mayor, B. R. Bernard Roundtree, J. B. Jim Thornburg and C. K. Charlotte Kellogg. (Courtesy of *The Pine Cone*)

been one of the promoters of the original gift of the land in 1910 by the Carmel Development Company, was elected mayor. He wasted no time in seeking to find a way that this unique theatre could be reborn. A request to the Depression-born WPA for a $20,000 grant for the reconstruction of the stage and seating was made and approved.

A year earlier an article in *The Pine Cone* should settle once and for all where Steinbeck got the name

Carmel's Forest Theatre as it appears today after its renewal as a WPA project in 1939. (Courtesy of the Harrison Memorial Library of Carmel)

'Tortilla Flat' for his story of that name. That article, titled "Tortilla Flat Affray" told how Andrew Gomez, popularly known as "Redwing", a swarthy native of Carmel, was struck by a knife in a late night tussle. His assailant was Jose Eturo, a Chileno who shared the house with Redwing at Santa Rita and First Ave, just inside the town limits of Carmel.

When a boat is wrecked in that story "on the rocks of Carmel" and the pile of flotsam is sold for five dollars Steinbeck may have visualized the rocks of Carmel Point as the setting for the shipwreck.

Carmelites were made aware of the growing threat to the peace of the world in 1938 when a "Letter From Spain" appeared on the front page of *The Pine Cone.* In that letter Dr. Leo Eloesser, a San Francisco doctor who was with the democratic forces

The 'Siren of the Rocks' at Carmel Point where Steinbeck set the shipwreck in his story *Tortilla Flat* (Photograph by Marguerite Temple)

in Spain, wrote of the primitive conditions for the care of the wounded in the Civil War that was engulfing that country. The connection of that conflict with the horror that the dictators were soon to bring on the whole of Europe was discussed in a talk given at the Carmel Woman's Club on "Dictatorship and Culture." And in December of that year Mrs. Frank Lloyd gave readers an insight into the emerging threat in an article for the paper, "Hitler Analyzed in the Light of His Life."

Bibliographical Notes

The history of the events which took place in Carmel during the period covered by this chapter are to be found in the filmstrips of *The Carmel Pine Cone* in the Harrison Memorial Library of Carmel. Fimlstrips of the other papers published in Carmel are also to be found there.

XI. Mission Rebuilding in the Second War Years

Carmel residents were in touch with the growing world problems as early as September 1934 when the Communist Party in the U. S. was refused permission to use the Sunset Centre Auditorium for a meeting. In the next year there were lectures at the Carmel Woman's Club on "Mussolini, Man and Monarch" and on "Hope for the Peace Movements."

And at the Filmarte Theatre there was shown a road show film entitled, "I was a Captive in Nazi Germany," depicting the experience of Isobel Steele in that country. An eyewitness account of the first bombing of Shanghai appeared in *The Pine Cone* followed by an editorial titled "Preparedness for War Seen Necessary."

In July 1939 an alternate sort of armament was urged at the Second World Assembly for Moral Rearmament held on the Monterey Peninsula. Delegates from all over the world assembled at Asilomar, being housed at Carmel and the other peninsula towns, to hear Dr. Frank Buchman make his plea for a moral rearmament which would make it possible to avoid war.

Buchman's hope that his MRA plan would solve the problems of the world and bring on a golden age of peace through a "God controlled" moral renewal proved to be a vain hope. Hitler invaded Poland and war was declared against Germany by Britain and France two days later.

Under the headline, "They've Gone to War!! Britishers Leave Carmel" it was announced that the many holding English citizenship were leaving Carmel to fight for their country. Their number included Lord Lionel Tennyson, grandson of the poet Alfred Lord Tennyson. Other Carmelites did their part in the British War Relief Festival that was held to raise money to support beds in an English hospital for wounded members of the Royal Air Force.

When the draft for the U. S. Armed Services was ordered 418 young men signed up and Carmel prepared itself for the possibility of air raids. Citizens volunteered to stand 2 hour shifts at night and 6 hour shifts by day to watch for and identify planes that would fly over the peninsula. It was soon after Pearl Harbor, on December 7th, that the Monterey Peninsula experienced a total blackout because of war fears. Instructions were given at the school, alerting Carmel students to proceedures in case of an air raid during school hours. The town's firemen were instruted in methods to control the effects of incendiary bombs..

An article appeared in the paper titled "City Mourns First Youth Lost in War" on May 1, 1942, relating how Gordon Bain, who had joined the R.A.F. before the U. S. entered the war, had gone down in his plane off the coast of Scotland. Later in the year a list of 200 men from Carmel who were in the armed services was in the local paper.

From that time until the end of the war in 1945 there was not a single issue of the paper which failed to carry an article about a Carmelite in the war zone or on leave at home, in hospital or killed in combat. Each issue carried advertisments, articles and cartoons urging support for the war effort.

Two hundred naval ratings came to live in Carmel in 1942 as overflow of those training at the Aviation Pre-flight School which had been established in the Old Del Monte Hotel after it had been taken over by the Navy. The hotel was never returned to civilian use but after the war was brought by the U. S. and today, with many additional buildings, is the Naval Postgraduate School.

The Carmel USO was popular with men from the army's Fort Ord as well as from the Naval School. And Carmel's theatrical know-how went into the war effort as the local production of "The Drunkard" toured the overseas camps under the auspices of the USO.

At home the shortage of tires and gasoline, both

rationed, cut down the number of tourists coming to Carmel with the result that many local merchants who depended on the tourist trade were forced out of business. Carmelites were told "What You Should Know About Rationing" and given suggestions in connection with the need for "Carmel To Raise Its Own Food."

SOMETHING ALL CAN DO

A cartoon that appeared in *The Pine Cone* on January 30th, 1942 which was representative of the cartoons, advertisements, articles that appeared in every issue, urging support of the war effort. (Courtesy of *The Carmel Pine Cone*)

It was during the war that the final exhumation and positive identification of the remains of Junipero Serra took place at the Mission San Carlos Borromeo which had been founded on the banks of the Rio Carmello in 1771. It had been in 1882 that Fr. Casanova, the rector of the Monterey Church who was holding occasional services in the ruined Mission building, discovered the burial.

He, with the custodian, Cristiano Machado, dug in the area of the sanctuary to find a stone-covered tomb. Below a broken part of the stone there could be seen a redwood coffin, partly filled with dirt, in which they found "remains in a splendid state of preservation." Realizing the importance of the discovery Fr. Casanova replaced the wood and stone covering until the whole area had been cleared of debris in preparation for a public opening of the tomb and those nearby. On July 3rd of that year a crowd gathered in the ruins of th Old Mission to witness the opening of the discovered tomb. In addition to the official church observors there was a contingent of St. Patrick Cadets from San Francisco along with many newspaper reporters and photographers.

A series of vaults was discovered in which were found four skeletons, each in a good state of preservation, with a stole in place on each. The stoles showed that these were indeed the remains of the three Franciscans, Serra, Crespi, and Lasuen, who had directed the Carmel Mission. The fourth vault held the remains of a young Franciscan, Lopez, who was at the Mission when he died.

The final and canonical exhumation and identification of the remains of Fr. Serra took place under the direction of Harry Downie, Custodian and rebuilder of the Carmel Mission, on september 1, 1943. For the occasion there were three official observers appointed by the bishop of the diocese together with Fr. Michael O'Connell, rector of the Mission Church, and two skilled anatomical physicians for the identification of the skeletons.

A bronze reliquary cross was found in the chest area of the skeleton in the central vault. This reliquary served to identify the remains in that tomb as those of Junipero Serra, for on the back of the cross were set nine relics of the blessed Raymond Lull, to whom Serra had shown special devotion. Downie placed the cross in the display case which he had made for the preserved portion of Serra's stole. He then set a mirror behind the cross so that the nine relics on the back of it can be plainly seen by the many visitors to the Mission Museum.

A view of the proceeding in the Carmel Mission ruins on the occasion of the uncovering of the vaults by Fr. Casanova on July 3, 1882. (Courtesy of the Harry Downie Collection)

Fr. Raymond Mestres, who succeeded Fr. Casanova at Monterey continued to take an active interest in the Carmel portion of his parish. Shortly before the outbreak of the first World War he had raised enough money to buy the part of the original mission land, now covered with the ruins of the old buildings, on which to rebuild the entire quadrangle of mission buildings.

The ruined adobe walls of the original mission buildings on the land bought by Fr. Mestress for his rebuilding project. (Courtesy of the Harry Downie Collection)

Plans for work on the mission restoration had to be shelved at the time of the entry of the United States into the war in 1917. After the war Fr. Mestres conceived the idea of creating a sarcophagus like those in European churches to hold the remains of Padre serra. For this he believed that he had found a sculptor worthy of the task when he saw in San Francisco's Golden Gate Park the heroic statue of Cervantes by Jo Mora who had his studio in Carmel.

The original plan was that the sarcophagus should be placed above the discovered graves in the chancel of the church. But as the design progressed it was evident that the work planned by Mora would be too large for that location. Plans were made to use the building to the left of the church entrance, for which ground had been broken, as a chapel to hold the sarcophagus.

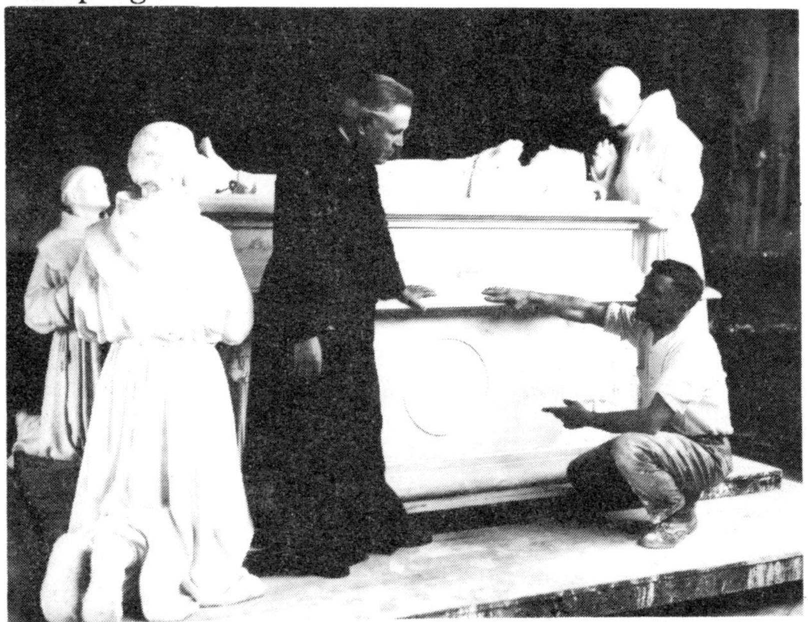

Fr. Mestres with Jo Mora as the plaster model of the Serra sarcophagus was being modelled. (Courtesy of the Harry Downie Collection)

By 1927 the sarcophagus and its chapel were complete and the greatest of the mission celebrations took the form of a 'Pilgrimage of Serra'. Preceded by a parade down Ocean Avenue of groups representing the three occupations of California - by Spain, Mexico and the United States a 'Fiesta de los Vaqueros' included a Spanish Fandango dance contest and horse races.

At the dedication the Duke of Alba represented the King of Spain and James Phelan, former Mayor of San Francisco and United States Senator, represented the United States President, while representatives from 21 missions founded by Serra laid wreaths. A large crowd came from the little village of Carmel and from Monterey and the surrounding towns as well as many San Franciscans and others at the Del Monte Hotel.

The ceremony at the dedication of the Serra Sarcophagus and chapel on October 11, 1927. (Courtesy of the Monterey County Library)

The Serra sarcophagus is one of the finest pieces of its sort to be seen in America and is on a par with the best that the European churches have to offer. It surprises some visitors that the remains of Serra are not in the sarcophagus but this is often the case in similar sculptured representations in Europe.

The rebuilding of the complete Carmel Mission took on a new impetus when Carmel became a parish in 1933 with Fr. Michael O'Connell as the first rector. Two years earlier a young man, Harry Downie, an experienced cabinet maker from San Francisco, had been appointed by the bishop to oversee the work. The two Irishmen, Downie and O'Connell, shared the planning of the restoration as well as the actual work of raising the adobe walls and placing the handmade roof tiles.

Harry Downie and Fr. Michael O'Connell working with a hired hand in the rebuilding of the Carmel Mission. (Courtesy of the Harry Downie Collection)

In preparation for his task Downie consulted all the sources available in order to be sure the restoration work would be correct in every detail. He searched through reports in Mexico and Spain of those who had visited the mission in its heyday. By excavation he discovered the foundations of the old building so that the reconstruction should follow exactly the line of the old buildings.

He completed the sarcophagas chapel, lining it

with the rich vestments of the padres sent to Serra and his successors from Mexico City, which he discovered to have been kept in the Monterey church. At the head of the chapel he placed the silver altar and processional crosses and silver candlabra along with Serra's silver chalice and paten which had also been preserved in the Monterey church.

The museum built around the Serra Sarcophagus contains altar fittings, gold and brass implements and vestments from the time of Serra and the other Franciscan fathers, Crspi, Palou and Lasuen. (Courtesy of the Harry Downie Collection)

He then built the rooms of the Padre's quarters adjacent to the Sarcophagus Chapel. These rooms, the old kitchen and dining room, Serra's cell and the mission library, give the present-day visitor a chance to see the padre's quarters as they looked in the eighteenth century. As a result of Downie's search and his purchase of books he found scattered throughout California the restored mission library now has 80 percent of the volumes collected by Frs. Serra and Lausuen.

Harry Downie working on plans for the mission rebuilding. (Photograph by John Livingstone)

Downie discovered the foundation stones and some of the remains of the wood of the cross that Serra raised in 1771 before the first crude chapel was built on the site. He replaced the cross with an authentic replica which stands today within the large patio of the school buildings which serve to replace the original mission buildings. He also raised crosses near the Carmel River and on the Monterey shore where they had been placed by Gaspar de Portola to mark landing places for ships from Mexico.

The climax to Downies's work in rebuilding was reached when, on February 5, 1960, a Papal Bull was issued by Pope John XXIII granting the title of Basilica to this mission church. A Basilica in a church of special historical and religious importance that takes precedence over all other churches but cathedrals. With the issueing of that Papal Bull the Mission San Carlos Borromeo in Carmel became one of twelve Basilicas in the United States.

The rebuilt Carmel Mission, the primary mission of the original California mission chain, as it stands today at the mouth of the Carmel Valley. (Courtesy of the Harry Downie Collection)

Harry Downie died on March 10, 1980, at the age of 76 after giving the last 49 years of his life to the service of the Carmel Mission and others of the California Missions which he supervised in the rebuilding. He is buried in the churchyard of his beloved mission.

With the end of the war the previous problems brought about by the lack of tourists were replaced by problems resulting from an overabundance of visitors. It was inevitable that so unique a place as Carmel should attract outsiders but as early as the summer of 1946 there was evidence of a sudden boom which was becoming a threat to Carmel-by-the-Sea as the oldtimners had known it as more and newer types of tourist serving shops multiplied.

One notable addition to the amenities of the town, the Carl Cherry Foundation, came into being as an indirect result of the war. Carl W. Cherry, a young graduate of the Massachusetts Institute of Technology and an inveterate inventor, had settled in Carmel before the outbreak of war. A wartime invention of his, "the Cherry Blind Rivet", which was said to have revolutionized the aircraft and ship building industry, brought him considerable wealth.

When Carl Cherry died of cancer at age 46 in 1947 his long time mate, the poet Jean 'Orge, established the Carl Cherry Foundation in one of the first houses built in the Carmel city development. In this building at Guadalupe and Fourth Avenue poetry readings and dramatic presentations are regularly provided to the benefit of Carmelites.

The open beach of Carmel from Pebble Beach to Point Lobos is enjoyed by all ages who live in or come to Carmel-by-the-Sea. The town has long protected its beach as a public park but beyond the city limits the beach was privately owned until the 1950s. Then, on September 3, 1950, it was announced that the City Council had appropriated $25,000 to be matched by the county and state for the purchase of the beach and lagoon from the end of the city limits to the lagoon at the mouth of the Carmel River.

From the time that the city had been incorporated in 1917 city offices were in rented quarters until the 1950's. In 1935 plans were made for a 'modern' city hall to replace Devendorf Park on

Ocean Avenue. Fortunately the bond issue for the new building was defeated by 328 votes to 198 at that time.

In 1951 the city bought the original church buildings of the Episcopal Church on Monte Verde when that church moved to its new location on Dolores. The old church building, built in 1912 for about $1,400, was remodelled to form the Council Chamber while the town offices were housed in the remodelled Parish Hall.

"I hear they run it just like a town. They have a mayor and everything." (A cartoon by Bill Bates, Carmel's resident cartoonist)

Then, in 1966 as the 50th anniversary of incorporation neared, a complex of municipal buildings was built at Junipero and Fourth Avenue for the Police and Public Works Departments. Included in the plans for the complex was modern a City Hall but, fortunately again, the City Hall portion was not built. In 1985 the original City Hall complex on Monte Verde was beautifully remodelled so that Carmel-by-the-Sea has now and for the future an attractive building that fits in well with the atmosphere of this unique town.

Bibliographical Notes

The definitive history of Mission San Carlos Borromeo is *The Carmel Mission, From Founding to Rebuilding* by Sydney Temple in which further bibliographical references are to be found at the end of each chapter. A copy of the most valuable thesis written by Sister Maria Celeste Pagliaril, Sisters of Notre Dame, is available in the Carmel Mission Library and at the Library of the University of San Francisco.

The history of events which took place in the period covered by this chapter can be found in the filmstrips of *The Carmel Pine Cone* in the Harrison Memorial Library of Carmel.

XII. A Heritage Town Offers Its Coastal Program

It was in 1971 that Gunner Norberg, a City Councilman, presented his plan for a 'Heritage City' in a four page supplement to the March 4th issue of *The Carmel Pine Cone.* Though most Carmelites have come here to get away from any kind of 'city', 'heritage' or not, they would all agree that they have found in Carmel what Norberg would call 'a human sanctuary'. From the time that writers fled from the ruins left by the 1906 San Francisco earthquake and fire to seek inspiration in the forested seaside resort this village has been a human sanctuary in a very real sense.

One of the Carmelites who fought most strongly to keep the different character of Carmel-by-the-Sea was Perry Newberry, an early mayor. He wrote of the town, "Nearly everyone that comes to Carmel wants the town to remain 'different' and hasn't the slightest conception of what its 'difference' is. Some people think it has to do with the holding back the town's population, being old-fashioned, keeping things primitive, getting along without the comforts and luxuries that modern life demands. NOT A BIT. The idea of holding back progress has nothing to do with the notion of keeping Carmel different, for difference, as far as the definition applies to our town means originality. Community originality is what has made Carmel a different town from its neighbors, and is what you found here that decided you to make it your home."

No longer do Carmelites have to get along without comforts and luxuries as they did in the early part of the 20th century, though there are no street lights in the older part of the town and most townspeople still have to go to the Post Office for their mail. But that is the way that the residents have decided that things should be. At the head of the basic zoning ordinance of 1929 the town was defined in a manner that the generations of residents before and after that time have fought to maintain, "Carmel is a residential community in which business and commerce have been, are now, and are proposed to be, subordinate to its residential character."

Norberg's words may sound strange to outsiders but Carmelites understood what he meant when he wrote, "Carmel is a city of the uncommon men and women, whether rich or poor or in between, who have an uncommon - but important care and concern for the place where they live." What is uncommon about the citizens of Carmel-by-the-Sea is that they have been successful in keeping their village unique enough to merit a title like 'a Heritage Town'. Even in the most recent period the town has remained 'different' despite the presence of two million tourists a year, the arrival of hundreds of new residents in the town and surrounding area and the election of a motion picture superstar as mayor in 1986.

One who lived in Carmel in the 1950's has in his cartoons shown an aspect of the simple life of any American neighborhood as he presents episodes in the saga of "Dennis the Menace." Hank Ketchum was resident in Carmel in 1951 when his first "Dennis the Menace" cartoon appeared.

Hank Ketchum with his son Dennis in their Carmel home in 1951 when the Dennis the Menace cartoons started. (Courtesy of the Weekend Magazine of the *Monterey Pininsula Herald*)

Ketcham, who has returned to live in the Pebble Beach area adjoining Carmel, tells of the episode which inspired the cartoon series. When the five year old Dennis was doing his usual thing at home one of his antics caused his exasperated mother to explode, "Henry, your son is a menace." Hank remembered that he repeated "Dennis - a menace" and that the idea then occurred to him that menace and Dennis rhyme nicely and might be an amusing title for a cartoon series.

"NOW CALM DOWN, HENRY! HOW WOULD HE KNOW IT WAS A TWENTY DOLLAR HAT?"

An early cartoon of Dennis the Menace that appeared March 30, 1951. (Courtesy of Hank Ketcham)

With his experience in drawing cartoons which had appeared in *The Saturday Evening Post* , *True*, and *Colliers* and as a Disney animator, he started to draw the "Dennis the Menace" cartoons for the daily newspapers.

While Carmelites were concerned with their local issues at this time, no neighborhood in America was untouched by the threat of the Polio epidemic. It was announced in *The Carmel Pine Cone* for April 2nd, 1955, that the county's allotment of Salk Polio vaccine had arrived. The receipt of this life saving vaccine had been held up because the need was greater in the southern counties of the state, the threat of an infantile paralysis outbreak being severe in the Los Angeles area. Within a few days shots of the vaccine were given to all first and second graders in the public, private and parochial schools in Carmel.

It was at this time that the City Council turned down the application of a nature group to set up a nudist colony in the Carmel woods. Perhaps it was a mark of the times that in August, 1955, a new local publication, *The Carmel Spectator Journal,* appeared which featured in its pages a series of artistic nude photographs and advertised itself as "The Nations's Unique Monthly." The reaction of the City Council to this threat to the town's reputation was to pass an ordinance that men must wear shirts on the city streets and women were to appear in bathing suits only on the beach.

Carved street signs were a feature of early Carmel and the most decorative of street signs was erected in 1957 to the last street to be added in Carmel. Red Eagle Lane, which runs between San Carlos and Mission Streets, was dedicated to one of the towns most colorful characters. Red Eagle, a Choctaw Indian born in 1870 in north Texas, had been adopted by Wild Bill Cody and at the age of 15 had begun to appear in the Wild West Show with rope spinning tricks. He came to Carmel in 1939 and lived in a little cottage at the back of the old Murphy Lumber Yard, located on Ocean Avenue, until his death ten years later.

Countess Claude Kinnoull affixing the street sign to mark Red Eagle Lane of January 9, 1957. (Photograph by Arthur MeEwen)

On January 9, 1957, a carved sign showing the head of an Indian wearing a feathered headdress was posted at the west end of that lane which was a sandy alleyway through which Red Eagle had passed on the way to his cottage. Countess Claude Kinnoull, a resident of Carmel and a longtime friend of Red Eagle, was given the priviledge of affixing the sign on the lane that was to honor one whom she described as "One of Carmel's citizens who has become an honored part of the City's legend."

At the same time that the Red Eagle sign was put in place there were carved squirrel and seagull signs on many of the street corners. Nearly all have now been 'lifted' and having seen so many of these carved street signs stolen by visitors the City Council decided to have the street names painted on the upright posts at street corners, together with the town's tree symbol. These remain because they are difficult to remove without the culprit being discovered and perhaps because they would have little value as 'collectibles'.

The type of squirrel and seagull street sign which once stood at many corners in Carmel. (Photograph by Marguerite Temple)

Though tourists support the town's economy, they do make problems as they crowd into the business district. Sometimes the sidewalks are so full of visitors that it seems as if there is no room for the natives.

Most of us who live either in the incorporated city of Carmel-by-the-Sea or in the area around the one square mile of the city limits came here as tourists before we returned to make it our permanent home.

A view of Ocean Avenue when the tour bus was still allowed on Carmel's main street. (Courtesy of *The Carmel Pine Cone*)

Therefore we can hardly complain about the tourists who come in even greater numbers since so much publicity has been given to the election of a motion picture star as mayor. Yet sometimes the natives feel like applauding what 'Claude' is shown as doing in a Cartoon by Bill Bates who was at one time Carmel's resident cartoonist.

In February, 1956 an extreme solution to the tourist problem was suggested by a citizens' committee which recommended the closing of Ocean Avenue to all vehicular traffic, making it a pedestrial walkway. This idea was turned down at first but the threat reappeared in the summer of that year when an outside 'town planner', Lawerence Livingstone, Jr.,

DAMN IT, Claude - we need a FEW tourists. (A cartoon by Bill Bates, Carmel's resident cartoonist)

presented his plan to the Carmel Planning Commission. His was a design for the complete transformation of the village aspect of the town. If his plan had been followed the center of town would have become a shopping mall of the sort that were springing up around the country, with a ring of motels around it, rather than the business district that had grown up through the years with motels scattered as they are now. At the head of Ocean Avenue a complete

Civic Center was to be built, closing off the main street, with traffic routed down Fifth Avenue to the beach. The state highway was to be moved so that all the through traffic on the highway would be routed along Junipero right into the town.

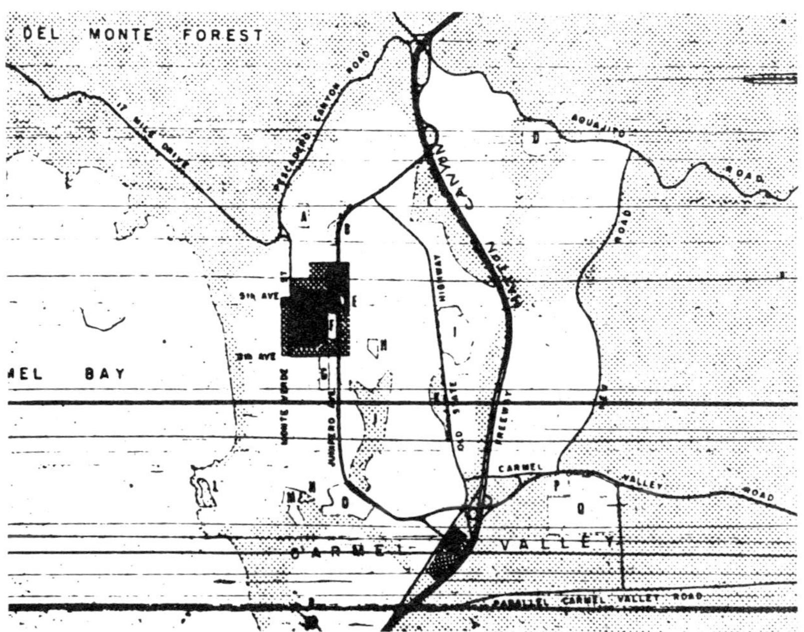

A sketch of the Livingstone general plan showing the reconstructed business and motel plan with Junipero as a main road into the city. (Courtesy of *The Carmel Pine Cone*)

With sketches of the suggested plan in *The Carmel Pine Cone* was an article by Wilma Cook, co-editor of the paper with her husband, Clifford Cook. Mrs. Cook argued that the plan "would change the character of Carmel and destroy the things that make it the distinctive and beloved community that it is."

Alongside was another article by Daisy Bostick, a long time resident and co-author of the only town history, *Carmel at Work and Play.* In this Miss Bostick asked WHY DON'T YOU STAND UP AND BE

COUNTED? against the plan. She wrote, "Sometimes I think I must be having a nightmare...If the plan is carried out to the bitter end there wouldn't be a smidgen of the real Carmel left."

The Carmelites did stand up to be counted and said NO to the plan in public meetings held that summer and fall. But the Planning Commission continued to consider the plan though it was stated that "If all the people who signed the petition against the plan stood shoulder to shoulder on Ocean Avenue they would reach from Junipero to the beach."

Throughout 1957 the plan was still under consideration by the City Council and it was not until December 19th of that year that an announcement could finally be made that the plan was definitely "thrown out". Thus was the greatest threat to this unique American community resisted by the determined action of its citizens.

In the same year the City Council contributed $3,700 toward the cost of a new prison in Monterey so that Carmel could continue to boast that it had no prison, no mortuary, no graveyard within its limits. The prohibition of street lights was decreed as was the cutting of any trees on (or in the middle of) any streets. 'Guest signs' are limited to 2 square feet per householder. Commercial signs, which must be approved by the City Council, are limited to 10 square feet with no moving parts and no use of neon lights.

There is one sort of threat to Carmel that no action by its citizens can defeat. Heavy Pacific Ocean storms have been a problem from the time that the first settlers came to the area. Together with high waves along the shore the storms bring heavy rain to the town and the valley above the town, causing the Carmel River to rise to flood level. In April of 1958 water poured into the Mission Fields district to the extent that 40 homes in the area bounded by Rio Road and Highway 1 were flooded. Despite night-long efforts to sandbag the river bank it was necessary for the Coast Guard to bring in rowboats to rescue some of the homeowners.

In 1960 the oceanfront window was broken out in the 'Butterfly House' which is located on the rocks on the ocean side of Scenic Road. As a result quantities of water swept through the house with the owner thrown against a chair in the Living Room as she fled the surge of water. After the storm the floors of the house were littered with boulders, sand and kelp, according to the report in the paper.

Carmel-by-the-Sea celebrated its Golden Anniversary in 1966. The Incorporation as a 'General Law City' having come in 1916. In that year a new Police Station was opened at the corner of Junipero and Fourth as the first unit of a projected Civic Center. After the Livingstone plan for a Civic Center to cut off Ocean Avenue was turned down new plans were made for such buildings on City land on Junipero and Fourth. Fortunately the City Hall was not moved to that location but the old City Hall was remodelled for continued use in the same old location. Only the Police Station part of the project was built together with space for the Public works division.

A photograph of the model of the Carmel Civic Center as designed by Burke, Shaw and Associates. The building to the left is the Police Station which is now built at the corner of Junipero and Fourth. Other buildings in the model are the City Hall to the rear and the Council Chamber to the right. (Photograph by Steve Crouch)

Instead of building a new City Hall as part of the complex at Junipero and Fourth the old City Hall was remodelled at a cost of $700,000 in 1984. A fine remodelling job was done but in that refitting the public seats in the City Council Chamber were reduced to 50 so that in 1986 it was necessary to move the monthly Council meetings to the Carmel Woman's Club building to accomodate the 200 to 250 people who attended the Council meetings.

Among the plans suggested for the City Hall was that of placing it at the site of the former Sunset School when it was purchasd by the City for $500,000 in 1963. But fortunately there was created there instead the unique Carmel Cultural Center for the scheduling of musical and dance concerts, plays and other special performances as well as the showing of classical motion pictures. The Center which has a full-time Director and staff is the focus of the annual Bach Festival and provides space for the offices of the Monterey County Symphony Orchestra and the gallery of the Friends of Photography. This latter is an important national association of photographers founded in 1967 by Carmel's world famous photographer, Ansel Adams.

The first causalty of a Carmelite in the Vietnam War was announced in November, 1969, marking the third time that Carmelites had gone to war for their country. The town, like the country, was to experience other problems of that difficult time. In the previous year a 25 hour Drug Crisis Center had been opened in town and in 1969 as many as 657 calls for help with drug addition problems were answered. This was also the time of the 'flowering' of the Hippie Culture and in 1970 it was estimated that 1,500 hippies were living in the area from the beach up the valley and along the coast.

When these problems were brought under control the City Councillors turned their efforts to the protection of the town's surroundings. The most ambitious plan was the Norberg Plan as outlined in a 4 page supplement to *The Carmel Pine Cone* for March 4, 1971. According to that plan a "Heritage City" was envisioned to include "at least the lands from the sea through the upper Carmel Valley to Jamesburg (30 miles inland), from Jack's Peak area to the north (near the Monterey airport) through the Carmel Highlands, down the coast and through Big Sur (25 miles south)."

There was nothing modest about the proposal. For a town that at different times had been afraid of "being citified like Pacific Grove" or of "Santa Cruzing its beach", the plan appeared to suggest a City and County of Carmel similar to the City and County of San Francisco. Though Norberg's vision of a "Heritage City" was too extreme, it did draw attention to the unique "Heritage Town" of Carmel.

In the one square mile of the incorporated city there are about 5,000 people, while in the 'Greater Carmel' area including the valley and Big Sur residents there are about 25,000. It is inevitable that with the two million tourists that come each year there would be growth in the commercial development in the central area zoned for business. By 1980 there were 900 retail and service businesses , or one for every four residents, and 940 rooms in the 50 motels and hotels, or one for every 5 residents. To care for the residents and short term visitors there are 60 restaurants while 40 real estate offices serve those who find that they want to become residents of this unique American community.

The city had 100 million in retail sales in 1985 compared with 21.5 million in 1970 but of the 3,000 business employees who flood the commercial zone each day only 11 percent are Carmelites. Yet the parking problems are kept under control with some new parking lots now established, more planned and 20 minute; green parking ares (with tire marking officers always on the prowl). The town keeps its unique style, boasting mainly quality shops such as I

Magin, the Lanz Stores, many boutiques and fine men's shops as well as 69 art gallery businesses and several establishments where fine antiques may be purchased.

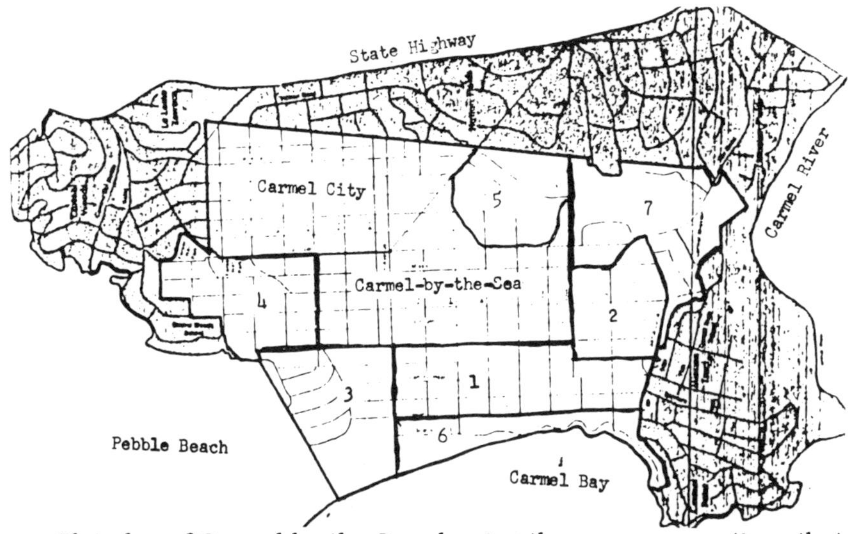

Plot plan of Carmel-by-the-Sea showing the seven annexations that have been made to the original 'Carmel City' and the unincorporated region surrounding. (Courtesy of *The Camel Pine Cone)*

There have been seven additions made to Carmel-by-the-Sea since it succeeded the failed 'Carmel City' development and incorporated as a city. The Ciity Councilors have been anxious to protect the environment of the town and it may be this that brought Monterey County to a place of leadership in the campaign to protect the California coastline. With the demise of the State Legistlature's Coastal Protection Bill in 1971 a group was formed that sought 6,500 signatures to an initiative petition to be offered to Monterey County voters. A year later the Alliance to Save the Coast was formed statewide to support a state initiative, Proposition 20, under which the State Coastal Commission was formed.

The proposals had opponents as well as

"No, Agnes, first He created heaven and earth...THEN He made Carmel." (A cartoon by Bill Bates, Carmel's resident cartoonist)

supporters. While Del Donte Properties contributed $15,000 for the campaign against the passage of the initiative, The Carmel City Council voted to support the proposition which was passed overwhelmingly by the vote of the people of California.

Six regional commissions were established under the provisions of the proposition to protect the 1,100 mile coastline. Monterey, Santa Cruz and San Mateo Counties come under the control of the Central

Regional Commission. Charles Kramer, chairman of that Commission, wrote in January, 1974 that the discussions of the Commission had often been "surrounded by controversy, lawsuits and red tape."

All would agree that there have been some questionable decisions in particular cases regardng the development of coastal property which have appeared to result in unfair restrictions on owners of property along the coast. Yet, as Mary Henderson, the next presiding officer of the commission, reported in 1976, "of the almost 2,000 permits processed in the Central Region about 95 percent have been approved." And anyone who has seen the development of the Honolulu or Florida waterfronts with walls of highrise apartments and hotels must be thankful that California has this Coastal Commission to protect its shores.

The destruction of the environment that even the Coastal Commission cannot protect the shoreline against are the terrible Pacific Ocean storms which batter the shore each winter. In 1983 one of the worst storms washed away the broad Carmel beach and waves which broke against the sea wall below Scenic Road undermined the pedestrian walk along the road.

Waves breaking against the foundations of the Frank Lloyd Wright house during the winter storms of 1983. (Photograph by Alan McEwen)

It was necessary for the City Council to appropriate $560,000 for the rebuilding of the seawall with 10,500 tons of 2 to 5 ton boulders to form a base for the renewed wall. And for that one year the annual Sand Castle Contest had to be cancelled.

The great Sand Castle Contest is generally held in September or October on the wide stretch of soft sand deposited by the calm summer sea. Originated in 1961 by Don Brown, a local rchitect, the annual event is sponsored by the Monterey Bay Chapter of the A. I. A.. The date of the event is never announced until a

The beach below Scenic Road when the Sand Sculptures Contest is held. (Courtesy of *The Carmel Pine Cone)*

few days before it is scheduled in an attempt to keep down the number of visitors who come. Yet as many as 5,000 people come to make or admire the sand sculptures from as far away as Texas and British Columbia.

The publicity that Carmel received in 1986 bids fair to bring visitors from even futher away. In the spring of that year the town was crowded with reporters and photographers not only from throughout the United States but even from throughout the world, when the motion picture superstar, Clint Eastwood, was running for mayor. When he was elected in April Carmel was seen on television screens around the world.

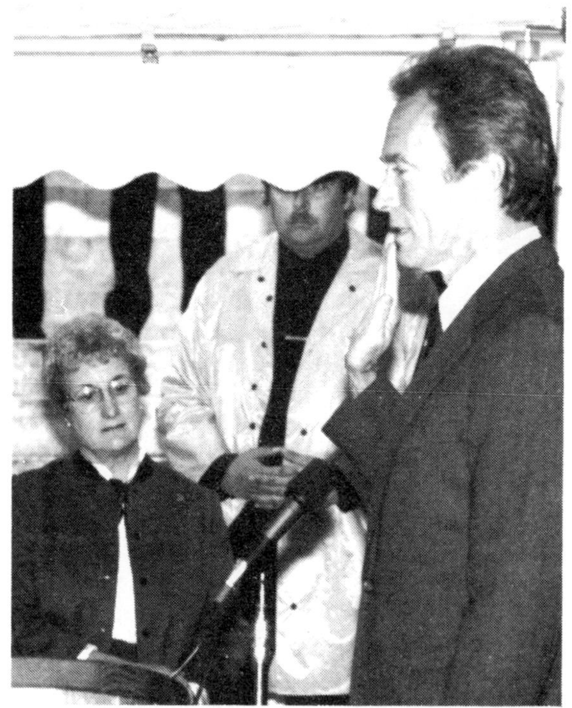

Clint Eastwood being sworn in as Mayor of Carmel-by-the-Sea (Photograph by Gregg Wutke)

As in any election there was a great difference of opinion and in this case there was the fear among the Carmelites that the election of such a well known person as Mayor might change the character of the town. Though it was necessary to move the monthly City Council Meeting from the 50 seat Council Chamber in the City Hall to the 250 seat Woman's Club auditorium to handle all who would attend the sessions, the fears appear to have been unfounded. The new regime has brought only much needed additions to the town's amenities including the reactiviating of the Carmel Youth Center.

Within the year several attractive and safe sets of stairs down to the beach from Scenic Road as well as the long planned public toilet building in one corner of Devendorf Park have been built. Temporary parking spaces have been made available on vacant city lots at Fifth and Dolores and Sixth and Lincoln. Plans are being made for a permanent underground parking garage at the latter location, part of which will be under the new addition to the Library. And studies are underway regarding a multistory parking garage in the area north of Sunset Center.

Tour busses, which have been limited to 20 minute parking on Junipero by the Plaza Shopping Center, are now allowed to remain for one hour so that the passengers may have some time to see a part of Carmel. Those who fear that this is a move by the business interests will be alert to the new plans for the community which are to be included in the rewriting of the General Plan.

That General Plan had to be formulated in agreement with Carmel's recently approved Local Coastal Program. By the Legislative Act passed in 1976 to replace the 1972 Coastal Initiative all 15 counties and 53 cities of the California coastline are required to file detailed coastal plans for the protection of the coastline in each are.

A Seagull's view of Carmel-by-the Sea

When Carmel-by-the-Sea presented its Local Coastal Program the city was granted certain "categorical exclusions" in recognition of the "strict and effective ordinances which protect and enhance the city's coastal environment", called "the strictest ordinance basis of any California community." Under its Local Coastal Program the enviroment of the city will be protected and under the rewritten General Plan its character as a unique Heritage Town will be preserved.

Bibliographical Notes

Because this is the first complete history of Carmel-by-the-Sea to be published the history of events covered in this chapter are to be found only in the film strips of *The Carmel Pine Cone* and a longer version of this work by the same author, in typescript, titled *Carmel-by-the-Sea, A Unique California Community*. Both can be found in the Harrison Memorial Library of Carmel.